"GENESIS AND THE MILLENNIUM"

An Essay on Religious Pluralism in the Twenty-first Century

by

Bill Moyers

Including Eight Ecumenical Responses

Marc H. Ellis
John Esposito
Stanley J. Grenz
Stanley S. Harakas

Martin E. Marty
Robert L. Millet
Sabrina P. Ramet
Harold Wells

Edited
by

Derek H. Davis

Published by the J.M. Dawson Institute of Church-State Studies
Baylor University
Waco, Texas 76798-7308
USA

GENESIS AND THE MILLENNIUM, AN ESSAY ON RELIGIOUS
PLURALISM IN THE TWENTY-FIRST CENTURY BY BILL MOYERS,
INCLUDING EIGHT ECUMENICAL RESPONSES

Address correspondence to
J.M. Dawson Institute of Church-State Studies
P.O. Box 97308, Baylor University, Waco, Texas 76798 USA

FIRST EDITION 2000

Library of Congress Cataloging-in-Publication Data
Preassigned Catalog Card Number: 99-69672

International Standard Book Numbers:
ISBN 0-929182-62-6 (PAPER)

CONTENTS

PREFACE

In the Fall of 1998, Bill Moyers came to Baylor University in Waco, Texas to deliver a lecture titled "Genesis and the Millennium." Not surprisingly, Baylor students turned out in significant numbers to hear him, in part because he is widely known across America as a popular and thoughtful producer, reporter, and author, but also because the high percentage of Baptist students at Baylor could proudly claim him as one of their own.

But Moyers was less anxious to speak to a group of fellow Baptists that day than he was to a group of friends—friends whom he knew were attentive to matters of faith, but like him, struggling to find the role of their faith in a world literally exploding with new and strange vistas of religious belief. The title of his lecture was drawn from his recently completed PBS Series, *Genesis: A Living Conversation*, a set of ten conversations centered on the Book of Genesis involving Moyers and a few dozen intellectuals whose professions ranged from scholar to poet, novelist to priest, artist to psychotherapist. Reflecting on those conversations, Moyers spoke of faith in the twenty-first century—of mainstream faith and of "weirdo" faith, of enlightened participation in politics and of outrageous participation, of liberal heresies and of fundamentalist heresies. But mostly he talked about learning to live together in a religiously diverse world, about how to "live learned lives of faith and value in a world where all of us must increasingly interact with people who are not like us." The lecture was at once conversation, warning, prescription, and plea. It was a message that could only be described as important. For many, it was a controversial message; it stirred no small amount of conversation on campus, to be sure. But all who heard the lecture knew it contained an important message that deserved some serious, ongoing conversation. This book responds to that impulse, to the felt need that more than just those who attended the lecture should be able to enter the conversation.

The conversation that takes place in this book is in the form of eight responses to Bill Moyers's lecture. The respondents represent primarily a wide range of Christian traditions, but Jewish and Islamicist responses are included as well. It is hoped that Moyers's lecture and the responses—a very stimulating conversation—will generate even more conversation among those who read them. The format seems ideal for classroom use, and this book was prepared with that forum principally in mind. But the book is certain to be profitable reading for anyone, particularly those who wish to reflect seriously on the impact of religious pluralism in America and elsewhere in the twenty-first century.

I wish to thank a number of people who have made this publication possible. Thanks are due to Robert B. Sloan, Jr., President of Baylor University, and Donald D. Schmeltekopf, Provost and Vice-President for Academic Affairs, Baylor University, for their enthusiastic support of this project. In addition, I am grateful to the members of the Beall-Russell Lecture Series Committee, Baylor University, headed by James Vardaman, who brought Bill Moyers to Baylor and then gave their permission to publish his lecture as the centerpiece of this book. Finally, a special word of thanks is due to Wanda Gilbert, who typed most of the manuscript, to Micah Watson, a graduate student in the J.M. Dawson Institute of Church-State Studies, Baylor University, who assisted with preparation of the manuscript for publication, and to Pat Cornett, for her expert editorial assistance in the final preparation of the manuscript and for coordinating publication details with the printer.

Derek H. Davis

ABOUT THE AUTHOR

Winner of more than 30 Emmy Awards and author of "Healing and the Mind," "Listening to America," and other bestselling books, Bill Moyers began his journalism career as a reporter at the *Marshall News Messenger* in Texas at age 16. Born in Oklahoma but raised in Texas, Moyers graduated from the University of Texas and later received the master of divinity degree from Southwestern Baptist Theological Seminary.

During his 25-year career in broadcasting, Moyers has been executive editor of the highly-acclaimed series, "Bill Moyers' Journal," senior news analyst for the CBS Evening News, and chief correspondent for the documentary series, "CBS Reports." Since establishing Public Affairs Television as an independent production company in 1986, Moyers has produced more than 200 programming hours including, "Facing Evil," "In Search of the Constitution," "God and Politics," "Joseph Campbell and the Power of Myths," "Amazing Grace," and "Healing and the Mind."

Moyers has been widely recognized as one of America's most insightful commentators. His honors include the Erik Barnouw Award from the Organization of American Historians; the George Foster Peabody Award for political reporting and international coverage; the Monte Carlo Film Festival's International Critics Prize; the National Endowment for the Humanities' Charles Frankel Prize; and the prestigious Gold Baton, which is the highest honor of the Alfred I. duPont/ Columbia University Award. He was one of the first three persons to be awarded the Honorary Doctor of Fine Arts by The American Film Institute. A survey of television critics by *Television Quarterly*, the official journal of The National Academy of Television Arts and Sciences, placed Moyers among the top ten journalists who have had the most significant influence on television news.

In addition to his 1971 best-selling book, *Listening to America*, four of Moyers's books based on his television series' have also become bestsellers. His many books include *Genesis: A Living Conversation; Global Dumping Ground: the International Traffic in Hazardous Waste; Healing and the Mind; The Language of Life: a Festival of Poets; What would you say to Thomas Huxley; A World of Ideas: Conversations with Thoughtful Men and Women about American Life Today;* and *The Ideas Shaping our Future, A World of Ideas II: Public Opinions from Private Citizens.*

Moyers's wife, Judith Davidson, an education specialist and corporate director, is his partner, creative collaborator, and president of their production company, Public Affairs Television, Inc. They have three grown children and currently reside in New York.

ABOUT THE EDITOR

Derek H. Davis, B.A., M.A., J.D., Ph.D., is the Director of the J.M. Dawson Institute of Church-State Studies, Baylor University, Waco, Texas, which offers M.A. and Ph.D. degrees in Church-State Studies, conducts research and publishes books on church-state relations and religious liberty in national and international contexts, and sponsors conferences and lectureships on various church-state themes.

In addition to serving as Editor of the award-winning *Journal of Church and State*, he is the author of *Original Intent: Chief Justice Rehnquist & the Course of American Church-State Relations* (1991) and *Religion and the Continental Congress, 1774-1789: Contributions to Original Intent* (2000), and is coauthor, editor, or coeditor of nine other books, including the *Legal Deskbook for Administrators of Independent Colleges and Universities*. He has also published extensively in various law and academic journals. His frequent magazine, radio, and television interviews have included those for *Time*, *The New York Times*, *The Washington Post*, *The Christian Science Monitor*, *The Los Angeles Times*, *Chicago Tribune*, *Wall Street Journal*, CNN, the Fox News Network, CBS News, and ABC News.

Genesis and the Millennium

BILL MOYERS

Thank you for inviting Judith and me to be here today. It's like coming home. When we were growing up in Texas—both of us in Baptist churches—Baylor University was the epicenter of our Baptist culture. Baylor lore was a rich vein in our heritage. Over in Marshall, where there were more Baptists than people, Baylor exes needed only the slightest excuse to repeat the story of how, when fire swept through the Carroll Library in 1922, students put themselves at risk to save most of the books, so greatly was learning valued. When I was a student at the University of Texas I once even proposed to friends that one day we put smoke bombs in the library there and rush out with armloads of books just to show that even infidels would risk for learning.

Baylor patriarchs were held up to us as heroes. Robert Emmett Bledsoe Baylor was one of them. He was the son of a captain in the Continental Army whose company served George Washington during the American Revolution. Baylor was converted in 1839 during a Baptist revival meeting in Alabama and moved to Texas where as a judge and preacher he traveled on horseback to enforce the law, holding court by day and preaching in the evenings. Fiercely devoted to learning and democracy, he helped to write the first Texas constitution which he made sure guaranteed free public schools and regular elections as essential to the new republic. As a founder of Baylor University he donated its first $1,000 and made sure it was located in a town appropriately called Independence, in Washington County. The history and character of this university were so profoundly shaped by this powerful mix of passions—for freedom and education, for religion and the law, for church and state (each honored but guarded from encroachment by the other).

Through the years Baylor's graduates have flowed into the churches, law firms, medical centers, businesses, classrooms, governments, and charitable organizations of Texas to create a vast infrastructure of influence felt in every nook and cranny of the state. You could get a solid education in the liberal arts here—symbolized by the presence on campus of the Armstrong Browning Library, one of my favorite places in the country—and you could also get a solid grounding in basic Baptist values through the presence of scholars like J. M. Dawson, whose groundbreaking work on religious freedom so deeply influenced my generation.

So Baylor was a mecca for many. Fathers sent their daughters to Baylor so they would be certain of graduating from college chaste, and mothers would send their sons here to chase them. Obviously every Baylor boy intended to marry a Baptist woman, but there were always some who would occasionally slip up to Dallas to first have some fun with a Methodist girl.

Given Baylor's reputation and influence, how was it that someone thoroughly reared as I was in a Baptist home and a Baptist church would end up graduating from the University of Texas? I could tell you that "The Devil made me do it!" But in truth the temptor was then Senator Lyndon B. Johnson, who offered me a job on his radio and television station in Austin at $100 a week, which despite its source was manna from heaven to someone working himself through school and yearning to get married in his junior year. Burdened by guilt over my errancy I fully intended in time to put things right by winding up at Baylor. So when (Baylor President) Judge Abner McCall offered me a teaching instructor's job at Baylor late in 1959 I immediately said yes, and Judith and I started packing. But before we could hit the road the devil struck again. LBJ called to say he was going to make a race for the Presidency and asked me to join his staff. Off we went to Washington. Abner McCall was no fan of the devil or of LBJ (frankly, he wasn't sure there was much of a difference) but he forgave my caprice and we remained good friends until his death, sometimes working together on issues of church and state. As for Lyndon Johnson, he never let me forget that the "B" in LBJ stood for his great-grandfather Baines: George W. Baines, Baptist pastor, teacher, and editor; friend of Sam Houston—and the third president of Baylor. He kept the young and hungry school alive during the Civil War, in the face of overwhelming financial obstacles and at great sacrifice to his health. Where he sowed, you reap.

It is true that like the prodigal son I journeyed into pagan lands. But today I've come home, and I am grateful to you— especially to Professor James Vardaman and the committee of the Beall-Russell Lecture Series—for this homecoming.

I

The eve of a millennium is a daunting time to try to make sense of things. "The Last Days Are Here Again" proclaims the title of a new book by Richard Kytle. The year 2000 is approaching, and apocalyptic fevers are rising. From pulpits to tabloids to bookstores, prophecies and predictions about the end of time have been a growth industry for years now. Christian fundamentalists tell us the second coming of Christ is imminent. They hear "the Four Horsemen of the Apocalypse—War, Plague, Famine, and Death—galloping toward Armageddon." New Age astrologers foresee psychic anguish, earthquakes, and economic collapse. Occultists warn of approaching calamities. Even President Reagan got into the act: "You know, I turn back to your ancient prophets in the Old Testament and the signs foretelling Armageddon and I find myself wondering if we're the generation that is going to see that come about. . . ." Never mind that it is the Book of Revelation and not the Old Testament that speaks of Armageddon. Apparently the source is immaterial if you have been seized by the apocalyptic vision. President Reagan's Secretary of the Interior, James Watt, and his Secretary of the Defense, Caspar Weinberger, both made similar statements, by the way, and for a time it seemed Doomsday might become national policy.

The exact timing of the end is anybody's guess, but here in Texas you may well be the first to know. According to a Texas-based organization called the House of Yahweh, sometime in the year 2000 four-fifths of the human race will perish as the world basically falls apart. Don't despair: the House of Yahweh offers a safe haven if you pierce your ears, change your name to Hawkins, and send 30 percent of your income to their Texas headquarters!

Through two thousand years of Western history millions of people have believed that they were living in the last days. It's as if a "dormant virus" resided in human genes that is activated when a millennium draws to an end. A thousand years ago the close of the first millennium since Christ produced waves of fear and trembling. Not everyone alive then was even aware that it was a millennium, of course. After all, the year 1000, like the year 2000, is a subjective date; no one really knows just when Christ was born. And the practice of numbering years consecutively throughout the Christian era wasn't even introduced until the sixth century, by a monk named Denis the Small, so reliance on the calendar was by no means universal when the first millennium came to an end. Many people slept through the great event the way I sometimes sleep through a Super Bowl which turns out far less exciting than the hype promoting it.

But many of the faithful aware of the first millennium were inflamed with an expectation that the "nightfall of the universe" was at hand, and they responded with spasms of anxiety. Christ was said to be coming again on the last day of the year 999, in Jerusalem, at the very stroke of midnight, and the roads to the Holy City filled with "an immense, desolating army" of pilgrims. Others were convinced the Antichrist would appear, precipitating a great battle between good and evil. Day after day, they "fearfully scanned the sky," expecting it any moment to be rent asunder. French nuns saw "fiery armies" fighting in the heavens. There were reports of fire-breathing dragons appearing in the clouds. Word spread of a mysterious disease known as St. Anthony's fire which ate away at the human body and soul. And when the sky rained blood—as it was described—people knew for sure they were entering a time of violence and warfare.

And so it was. Europe warred with invading Muslims, Bulgars, Magyars, and Vikings. Conditions within Christendom so appalled the Archbishop of Rheims that he wrote of men who "lived without law and fear of punishment, abandoning themselves to their passions." Carnage, famine, cannibalism, pestilence, murder, and madness plagued the continent. Corruption ran rampant in high places. Popes and kings plotted each other's assassination. And as the fateful year 1000 approached, their hearts and minds gripped by nightmare visions, many good Christians "knelt trembling in their churches, waiting for the last trumpet to sound, shedding so many tears of repentance that they ran down their legs, even to the toes."

Now, all this may sound to you just like another Phil Gramm political campaign, but you can read all about it in a splendid little book entitled: *AD 1000: Living on the Brink of Apocalypse* by Richard Erdoes. No doubt it will soon be coming to a theatre near you starring Arnold Schwarzenegger and Bruce Willis.

Not surprisingly, as we approach the third millennium, even the most resolutely secular of sensibilities will probably find itself being sucked into the collective cloud of hope and foreboding, the wavering of faith in human institutions, the tendency to sudden panic that humanity has always been prone to display when it has felt a new era coming on. And it's not only Christians who get caught up in the fervor. Believers in other faiths talk of the coming of the anointed Messiah, of the Mahdi, of the Tenth Imam, even of Buddha. And a small group of neo-Nazis—no doubt longing for the thwarted advent of a thousand-year Reich—awaits the reappearance of Adolf Hitler, reportedly on his way back to earth this very moment from the planet Zeno.

The Economist calls it PMT—that "pre-millennial tension" which provokes people to the most dire interpretation of events, from convulsions on the sun to mass murders in Waco or at Heaven's Gate in California. Whatever we call it, let us take a deep breath and count to ten, remembering that, as William Penn once said, "to be furious in religion is to be furiously irreligious." Baylor's strong historical traditions, and its influence not only in religious but secular circles, make this an ideal place for the calm and deliberate examination of what it means to be religious in a modern democracy, in a society undergoing unprecedented transition at a time of greatly charged sensibilities. You have set an example for us in your recent and successful efforts to prevent the takeover of Baylor by those reactionary forces that have seized control of the Southern Baptist Convention and turned its institutions from education to indoctrination. The life of the mind and the life of the spirit are strongly linked at Baylor, and neither the hot frenzy of hysteria nor the cold blade of conformity must ever be allowed to sever them.

Nor can you surround yourself with a moat. Even when I first visited Baylor there were more than thirty denominations represented on the campus. Such ecumenical hospitality thrives to this day, making this a community where it is possible to reflect on how best to prepare young people to live learned lives of faith and value in a world where all of us must increasingly interact with people who are not like us.

Judith and I dealt with this challenge in our recent PBS series on Genesis. I know some of you saw that series because you wrote me about it at the time. There were ten broadcasts over ten weeks, each devoted to one of the great stories from the first book of the Bible. A simple series, by television's standards. Seven people, facing each other in a circle of conversation, the way our ancestors sat around the campfire. A simple series, to be sure, but none of our work on television until then had created more media response prior to broadcast than those ten discussions of Genesis. All over the country people organized into groups so they could watch the programs together and then talk about them afterwards. One organization alone signed up a million people just for this purpose. We think this enthusiastic reaction has implications both for democracy and for our individual and collective response to the approaching millennium, as I trust to have made clear by the time our visit this afternoon has ended.

II

What I'd like to do is talk a little about the background of the series, share some impressions of what I think—and hope—we accomplished, and then briefly mention our hopes for what might come from such an effort.

I'll confess to you that I'd long wanted to produce a book whose jacket announced that between these covers is an earthy and violent saga of sin and sex, violence and murder, love and betrayal, plagues and calamity, cruelty and compassion, visions and hallucinations. But . . . mother wouldn't let me, and God beat me to it. So we did the next best thing; we made a television series based on the book of Genesis.

We wouldn't have done that, however, if we hadn't first heard about a Genesis seminar being conducted near our home in New York at the Jewish Theological Seminary of America, the academy of conservative Judaism in this country. Once a month a young Rabbi had been gathering an assortment of novelists and poets, editors and screen writers, and biblical scholars—both Jewish and Christian—to work their way, word by word, verse by verse, story by story, through the book of Genesis, in a spirit of candor, curiosity, and openness. A *New York Times* reporter sat in on the sessions and called it "the best conversation" in town. When I called Rabbi Burton Visotzky to ask if Judith and I could attend some of his sessions, he invited us to the very next session.

It was our first exposure as Baptists to the Jewish tradition of midrash. So let me pause and share what we learned about it. The word "midrash" comes from the Hebrew word meaning to seek out, to search out, to inquire. It's a process of creating imaginative responses to specific biblical texts. First practiced by rabbinic sages in the Roman period, over the centuries midrash came to be used by biblical scholars, literary theorists, and ordinary readers alike. To do midrash is to fill in the blanks in the biblical text—to puzzle over ambiguity and nuance, speculate on the motivation of characters, play with puns.

For example, a midrash might speculate on what Sarah was actually thinking when her husband, Abraham, took their slave, Hagar, to bed. This had been Sarah's idea. She and Abraham were supposed to have a child who would become the seed of the covenant, but at 90, still barren, the covenant still in doubt, she suggested that Abraham impregnate Hagar, to produce a child with her—the first surrogate mother, if you will. But what was Sarah thinking when the consummation took place? The Bible is silent here. Midrash addresses the silence, teasing out of the text its hidden meanings through a vigorous give-and-take of interpretation.

Watching this engaging group of people reading fresh meaning into the ancient words, I was soon caught up in their intellectual and spiritual energy. There was lots of passion, many disagreements, but always civility and good humor reigned. People were wrestling with the text as if it really mattered. And they were listening to each other. I was reminded that "conversation is the art of hearing as well as being heard." I was also reminded of what John Drakeford had called "The Awesome Power of the Listening Ear." These people were really listening to each other. Sitting like a fly on the wall in that first session we attended, I remembered our first visit to the great French cathedral in Chartres: that magnificent Gothic structure that sweeps one's fixation up toward the grandeur of God. Turning a corner I came upon a sculpture so stunning it stopped me in my tracks. The artist depicts Adam, the first human, emerging as an idea from the side of God's head. God is literally *thinking* us into existence. I was struck, standing there, by the realization that if we human beings are indeed imprinted with the image of God, possessing a Godlike creative faculty, surely we were intended to use our minds to *think* . . . to speculate upon and debate the implications of existence, including our own understanding of faith and scripture . . . to argue, if you will, with the text itself, even with the Creator himself.

And that was happening in the Genesis seminar. One of Rabbi Visotzky's favorite moments occurred when participants were discussing God's command in Genesis 12, where Abraham is told "to go from your land and your birthplace and your father's house and I will show you a new land and make you a great nation." After the Rabbi read the text, Max Apple, the novelist, who teaches at Rice University, spoke up quietly and said, "I wouldn't have written it that way." They all looked at him. And Max Apple, rather sheepishly, said, "No, it's not a test of Abraham's faith if he's promised a reward from the very start." This triggered a lively and vigorous discussion, because it was not only a valuable commentary on the story, it also liberated the participants to respond to the scripture with their own intellect and from their own experience.

We had an intuition, Judith and I, that this would make good television. It took us some time to raise the money—longer by far than it took God to create the whole universe—but we finally succeeded. We kept hearing that Americans didn't want to hear God-talk on television. Perhaps this explains why, although nine out of ten Americans tell George Gallup they've never doubted the existence of God, it's hard to hear God mentioned in mainstream media except by somebody who's trying to put something over on you. William F. Buckley has said that if you mention God once at a dinner in New York, you'll be greeted with silence. But if you mention God a second time, you'll never be invited back. We wanted to test that idea, to see if people would come back week after week to hear other people talking publicly about God.

Our most critical step was to select the participants. The Bible is a closed book, unless you read it with an open spirit. So we looked for people who had a real commitment to the Bible but who brought with them a quality of openness. Thomas Moore says conversation is "the interpretation of worlds." The reason I like to interview people is because they provide me a passport into worlds I'd never enter without their help. Talking with people who agree with you is like jogging in a cul-de-sac. When I was growing up in East Texas, Baptists talked about the Bible with Baptists, Presbyterians with Presbyterians, Episcopalians with Episcopalians, Methodists with Methodists, Jews with Jews, but we never talked about the Bible across our faiths, not to mention with other races. Marshall was 50 percent black and 50 percent white and yet our two communities never got together to talk about and interpret our worlds to each other.

So we wanted to be sure our participants in the series didn't come from the same neighborhood. We sought out people from different backgrounds, faiths, professional fields, age, and gender. One of my own criteria was that each person had to be someone I wouldn't mind being stranded with somewhere waiting rescue—and each of our participants fit the bill. Our final lineup included visual artists, a literary critic, novelists, theologians, biblical scholars, a journalist, an editor, ministers and rabbis, a college president, a clinical psychologist, two Muslims, a Hindu writer, a musician, and a Republican. (Just kidding: I wanted to see if you were paying attention.)

We couldn't have had better material. Genesis offers the power of great storytelling. The power of characters as complex as any you'll ever meet in literature. The power of a divine presence in the shaping of a people. Three great faiths trace their origins to these stories. They are the quintessential Jewish story. We Christians have adopted them to our canon. And Muslims trace their beginnings back to the departure from Abraham's camp of Hagar and the child Ishmael born of their union. For three faiths Genesis is a documentary of the founding generation. And yet, these very old stories speak across the generations with a relevance that is almost staggering to me.

One reason is because their characters are starkly human. They rage at one another and at God. They're schemers and dreamers and parents who play favorites and children who run away from home. Here are tales of willful sons and estranged brothers and troubled marriages. Lots of envy, lust, infertility, deception. All of the elements we would describe today as a dysfunctional family. These are people like us, you see, which is why they confront us so directly today.

Let me give you a couple of examples.

The Story of Noah. If you saw this program when it aired, you know we were forced to wrestle with some troubling issues. When I was a kid in Sunday School at the Central Baptist Church in Marshall, we didn't have baseball cards, we had Bible cards depicting scenes from the scriptures. The Bible card with Noah I remember especially. Mr. and Mrs. Noah, sitting on the prow of the Ark, gazing out toward the horizon at the beautiful rainbow arching across the sky. All the animals—the anteaters, antelopes, and aardvarks—gathered around with little smiley faces. The perfect children's story. A real American story with a setting and ending suitable for Walt Disney.

But this is no children's story. It raises hard questions about adult behavior. If Noah knew what was coming, why didn't he alert his neighbors—or at least his in-laws? The fundamentalists will tell you it was because Noah was just being obedient to God. He was just doing what he was told.

But we have to ask: Does obedience carry with it the negation of mercy? Was there no pity in his heart for those in the path of the flood? Was he so intent upon establishing the first chapter for the Society for the Prevention of Cruelty to Animals that he didn't have any concern for his fellow human beings?

Those of you who saw our discussion will remember that one of our participants, Karen Armstrong, reminded our group that the original title of the novel on which *Schindler's List* is based is *Schindler's Ark*. Thomas Keannelly, who wrote the book, thought the image of the Ark was appropriate for Oscar Schindler's factory, where he saved hundreds of intended victims of the Nazi Holocaust. Now, Schindler was no righteous man in the conventional sense of the word. He was a playboy and a philanderer—the kind of fellow God would probably have drowned back in Noah's day. And yet, Oscar Schindler risked his life to rescue the doomed and the damned. Most of his contemporaries behaved like Noah. They blocked out all knowledge of the carnage, obeying their superiors in order to save themselves, trying to ride out the storm in safety. I was confronted during that discussion by a very hard question: If I had been raised in Munich, Germany, instead of Marshall, Texas during the early thirties, would I, as a Christian, have tried to save anyone?

These stories present us with tough questions. What are we to make of Noah's conduct after the flood? He was clearly traumatized when he got off the boat. The first thing he did was to build an altar. Now when I was young we were told this confirmed his righteousness—proving he deserved to be saved. But just a few verses later, Noah gets drunk, curses his children, and abuses his grandson. No sooner does God save this man, giving humanity a second chance, than the rainbow fades into alcoholism and child abuse. Tough questions, indeed. In many ways, I've come to think of Noah as the quintessential twentieth-century figure. In the Jewish mystical teachings, the Kabbalah, the world never really escaped the devastation of the flood. It represents, metaphorically, the dilemmas of contemporary society. Its waters rage all around us—and within us, as well.

And what about God in this story? I was taught that when God saved Noah, he was showing compassion. But Jack Miles paints a different picture. Miles won the Pulitzer Prize for his book, *God: A Biography*. And Jack Miles tells us this is not the story of a good God saving a good man from a natural disaster. This is the story of a good God saving a good man from a bad God. And the horror of the story is that the good God and the bad God are the one and the same God.

Remember, in the first chapter of Genesis, not once but seven times God says of creation, it's good. But just six chapters and ten generations later, God is so appalled by the violence and the corruption of humanity that God drowns everyone except for Noah and his family and the animals they could get on the Ark. Now, surely there were children on earth too young for corruption. What does it say that we have come to revere a story that has no place for the innocent bystander? The God of Genesis, says Jack Miles, is a God of radical unpredictability, combining immense physical power with terrifying moral ambivalence.

We get here, in the silences of this text, the question which haunts our own genocidal century. Why must the innocent suffer? And how is it faith survives events that contradict it? One of our participants in the series told of the Jews condemned to die in the concentration camp at Auschwitz. Day after day they are marched into the gas chambers to die. But one day the survivors decide they've had enough. They decide that God must be tried for having let all this horror happen. So they convene a tribunal. They hear all the evidence. They pass their judgment. They pronounce God guilty and they sentence God to die. No sooner than the judgment is rendered than one old rabbi gets up and says, "Alright, the trial is over. It's time for the evening prayer."

I wrestle with that contradiction: "I believe; help thou my unbelief!"

The Story of Cain and Abel. If you saw our series, you may remember that one of our most fascinating discussions was around the story of Cain and Abel. You know the story: Adam and Eve are the first parents to discover what it means to raise Cain. They have a second son named Abel. Both boys want to please God so both bring God an offering. Cain is a farmer and offers the first fruits of the soil. Abel is a shepherd and offers the first lamb from the flock. Two generous gifts. God, playing favorites, chooses Abel's offering over Cain's, and the elevation of the younger leads to the humiliation of the elder. Cain is so jealous he strikes out at his brother and kills him.

Here is the first paradox we confronted in our discussion: Abel is innocent and yet Abel dies. If you saw the broadcast you know that at this particular point, the novelist, Mary

Gordon, a struggling Catholic, says, "This is the hopeless moment. The realization that goodness and purity do not protect you. It did not protect the Jews. It did not protect the Africans sold into slavery. It did not protect the Native Americans. Goodness and purity of heart," she said, "are irrelevant to your fate and punishment. In the end, Abel is dead. And dead is dead, and God did nothing about it." This is the narrative moment, says Mary Gordon, "when doubt becomes absolutely comprehensible and almost inevitable." But she goes on to express poignantly what it means to be a survivor. Mary Gordon says the challenge for a moral person is always to be a witness to Abel. To be an ethical human being, she believes, is to say, "I'm in the place of that person unjustly cut down. I am a witness to that." All of us who are survivors at the end of this genocidal century are confronted by that imperative: What can I DO to put things right, to assure it never happens again? To what will my life witness?

Here's the second paradox. The first murder arose out of a religious act. Both brothers are rivals for God's favor. Their rivalry leads to violence and ends in death. Once this pattern is established, it's played out in the story of Isaac and Ishmael, Jacob and Esau, Joseph and his brothers, and down through the centuries in generation after generation of conflict between Muslims and Jews, Jews and Christians, Christians and Muslims, so that the red thread of religiously spilled blood runs directly from East of Eden to Beirut to Bosnia to Belfast— to every place in the world where the compassion of brothers and believers, of sisters and seekers, turns to competition and violence.

As James Wiggins says in *In Praise of Religious Diversity*, virtually every armed conflict that is occurring on the planet today is explicitly driven by religious motives or by memory traces of persisting religious conflict. So we get Sunni Muslims in Afghanistan fighting a civil war with Shiite Moslems. We get fundamentalists in Algeria who want to make their country an Islamic theocracy, shooting teenage girls in the face for wearing a veil and cutting professors' throats for teaching male and female students in the same classroom. We get Muslim suicide bombers killing busloads of Jews. And a fanatical Jewish doctor with a machine gun mowing down thirty praying Muslims in a mosque. We get the young orthodox Jew who assassinated Yitzhak Rabin, declaring on television, "Everything I did, I did for the glory of God." In India Hindus and Muslims slaughter one another. Here in

America, Muslims bomb New York's World Trade Center in order to smite the Great Satan. Timothy McVeigh blows up the Federal building in Oklahoma City, killing 168 people, in part as revenge against the government for killing David Koresh and his followers. Groups calling themselves the Christian Identity Movement and the Christian Patriot League collect arsenals, and at a political convention in Dallas not long ago, at a so-called "Christian" booth in the exhibit hall, you could buy an apron with two pockets—one for the Bible and one for a gun. "To be furious in religion is to be furiously irreligious."

Religion has a healing side, we know this; but religion also has a killing side. From Genesis "the voice of thy brother's blood cries out to me." In our television discussions of Cain and Abel Mary Gordon also said, "It's quite remarkable I'm not behind bars. I find trying not to be a murderer completely grueling." We laughed. But she made us consider how superficial is the veneer of civilization that stretches over the passions of the human heart; how, within each of us, the tendencies to do good conflict with the opposing inclination.

What is it about our species? Soon after taping the series we visited our grandchildren in Minnesota. It was early and I was up alone having coffee in the kitchen, reading the newspaper, when young Thomas, who was then two, came down. Thomas likes his cereal straight. So I poured his Cheerios out on the high chair and he sat there eating as intermittently we talked while I read and he amused himself with his cereal and imagination. About half an hour later Henry, who was four, came down. Henry, the gentle blue-eyed child with the sweet and sensitive face. He comes into the room, he sees his younger brother; he doesn't say, "Hi, Thomas" (or "Morning Pa"). He says, "Thomas, I'm going to kill you." Now, this is a family where watching television has been strictly restricted. He didn't hear this kind of talk from his parents or his grandparents. Where did the notion come from? What is this primal impulse that can surface so quickly to wither a brother? We struggle as a society in choosing which side of our nature we're going to nurture.

These stories don't always have happy endings or provide easy answers. They force us to confront our own quandaries without pat solutions. When I was a child the characters in the Bible were ten feet tall. In seminary I studied the stories for the purpose of learning the answers to questions I would be asked later in classrooms or by congregations. But life has a way of questioning your answers; bumper sticker theology and sound bite philosophy cannot tell me what I need to know. I see myself reflected in these people of Genesis. They don't always do the right thing. They don't always even know what the right thing is. They live with ambiguity. Very often, they don't know what to make of God and, quite often, God doesn't know what to make of them, either.

III

So why do a series like this, if you can't offer people answers to their questions?

For one thing, we hoped the series might make a difference in people's lives. James Wiggins writes that most of us see the sacred spiritual journey as a part of our potential; it tells us who we are. These stories are part of that journey for millions of people. So we hoped the series, in a modest way, would encourage viewers to enlarge their thinking about the world, to seek perspectives that go beyond their own, to make connections where none existed before.

Above all we wanted to see if it's possible to talk about God in public without politicizing religion or polarizing the community. We hoped to show that you can disagree passionately with people about things that matter without surrendering your own principled beliefs or going for your neighbor's throat; that we can engage with others in serious conversation about the most deeply felt subjects—our religious belief, the nature of faith, our relationship with others—and truly challenge each other, teach each other, and learn from each other.

Why is this important? Because we're entering a new religious landscape in America. Diana Eck recently reminded us that for most of our history this country's religious discourse was dominated by white male Protestants of a culturally conservative European heritage, people like me. Their core values went largely unchallenged. Dissenting visions of America, alternative visions of faith, of race, of women, rarely reached the mainstream. Just the other day a friend on the West Coast sent me a clipping from the cartoon strip, *Shoe*. Two weirdos are talking in a California diner. One weirdo says to the other, "Have you ever delved into the mysteries of Eastern religion?" And the second weirdo answers: "Yes, I was once a Methodist in Philadelphia." Once upon a time that was about the extent of our exposure to the varieties of religious experience. But it's different now.

When I moved to New York in 1968, I was impressed to see people on the subway reading the Hebrew Bible. I'd never seen that in Marshall, Texas. I was impressed to see people on the subway reading the Bible in Spanish. Never saw that in Marshall, Texas. When I ride the subway today, I'm just as likely to see someone reading the Koran as I am the Bible. There are more Muslims in America than Episcopalians or Presbyterians. And within a few years there may be more Muslims in America than Jews. I read one day that Muslims are the fastest growing religion in America. Then I read that Pentecostals are the fastest growing religion in America. Then I read that the fastest growing Christian denomination is the Church of Jesus Christ of Latter Day Saints, Mormons—doubling in number every fifteen years since World War II.

Our nation is being re-created right before our eyes. Travel the country and you see an America dotted with mosques—in places like Toledo, Phoenix, Atlanta. We have huge Hindu temples—in Pittsburgh, Albany, California's Silicon Valley. There are Sikh communities in Stockton and Queens, New York, and Buddhist retreat centers in the mountains of Vermont and West Virginia. A Buddhist American died on the Challenger. A Muslim American is the mayor of a small town in Texas. Hindu Americans are now managers at Boston Edison and Proctor and Gamble. "The world is shrunk," and we cannot avoid the claims of different stories and ideas impinging upon us. Because every religion conveys possible ways of expressing human existence and self-understanding, and because each can appear utterly incomprehensible to the other, we are facing what Gerald Bruns describes as a "contest of narratives." There are more meanings "than we know what to do with. . . . We are like Odysseus, accumulating more stories than we could possibly want, but not too many to tell."

Now, the dictates of democracy govern America both politically and culturally. We not only tolerate but celebrate diversity, in principle if not always in practice. But we ain't seen nothing yet! As the world's religions take root here, can they co-exist peacefully? What is our response when we discover that the followers of another faith believe their religion is superior to others—the sole bearer of the truth about God? How do we avoid the intolerance, the chauvinism, the fanaticism, the bitter fruits that occur when religion is used as a wedge to drive people apart?

It's no rhetorical question. At one point in our series the scholar Elaine Pagels said, "There's practically no religion I know of that sees other people in a way that affirms that other's choice." Even within denominations this is so. Like the siblings in Genesis, different factions of one religious family may no longer speak to each other, except through clenched teeth. Baptists, for example.

At last count, there were more than two dozen varieties of Baptists in America. I'm a Baptist. So is Pat Robertson. Bill Clinton is a Baptist. So is Newt Gingrich. Al Gore is a Baptist, and so is his rival, Richard Gephardt. Jesse Jackson is a Baptist. So is Jesse Helms. No wonder Baptists have been compared to jalapeno peppers: one or two make for a tasty dish, but a whole bunch of them together in one place brings tears to your eyes.

We Baptists differ profoundly in how we read history; how we read the separation of church and state; how we read election results. Baylor was founded by men steeped in the stories of colonial America when Baptists were fined, flogged, and exiled for refusing tribute to official state religions. In Massachusetts, in 1651, the Baptist Obadiah Holmes was given thirty stripes with a three-corded whip just for taking communion with another Baptist who was elderly and blind. Holmes refused the offer of friends to pay his fine so that he could be released. They offered him strong drink to anesthetize the pain, but he wouldn't take it. Sober, he endured the ordeal; sober still, he would one day write: "It is the love of liberty that must free the soul."

That idea took root in America and eventually put an end to the power of magistrates to order citizens to support churches they did not attend and recite creeds they did not believe in. It was this conviction about the moral exercise of conscience and the independent prerogatives of church and state that made America "a haven for the cause of conscience."

Now, Baptists of Pat Robertson's stripe seem to have a different idea about that than the rest of us. Pat Robertson calls the separation of church and state "a lie of the left" and vows to dismantle it. I hardly need remind you this is the same Pat Robertson who said Jews are "spiritually deaf" and "spiritually blind"—who compared non-Christians to termites "destroying institutions that have been built by Christians."

I find it curious that Baptists of that stripe invoke the separation of church and state to protect themselves against encroachment from others but denounce it when it protects others against encroachment from them.

They use it to shelter their own revenues and assets from taxation, but then insist taxes be paid by others to support private sectarian instruction in pervasively religious schools.

They loathe any government intrusion into their sphere, but labor mightily to change federal tax laws so that churches may more easily influence government.

They stand foursquare behind the First Amendment when they exercise their own right to criticize others—sometimes with a vengeance and often with vitriol. But when they in turn are challenged or criticized, they whine and complain that their critics don't respect them as "people of faith." I couldn't believe my eyes one night watching C-Span: There was Newt Gingrich rousing the Christian Coalition to a fever pitch of paranoia by telling them they are victims of "Christian-phobia." This in a country where the President, the Vice President, the Majority Leader of the Senate, the Speaker of the House, and the Minority Leader of the House are all—Christians!

But remember: Gingrich was speaking to people who act as if the Bible belongs to them. They would have us concede they speak for God when they bring their opinions to bear on all kinds of political issues—from abortion to the environment to the public funding of the arts. When you challenge them, they cry "foul"—as if your disagreement with them is a form of persecution. That's absurd, of course. In a democracy, no one can simply claim the higher ground of morality without defending it. And just because your opinion is based on religious experience doesn't make it unarguable.

For too many years now the religious discourse in America has been dominated by the religious right, amplified by media which seem to regard fundamentalists as the only authorities around on the subject of religion and society. Not surprisingly, religion in official Washington has come to be just another political action committee, like the National Association of Manufacturers or the National Rifle Association—Moses and Jesus in Guccis prowling the corridors of power, advocating tax breaks for their clients!

Frankly, I'd like to see a wide embracing coalition of people from across denominational lines—people who care deeply about the sacred texts and also understand that others

who read them differently care deeply about them as well—
I'd like to see us take the scriptures back from the grip of
those who assert an exclusive pipeline to God.

Our series showed it can be done. The conversation was
notably enriched because we didn't all come from the same
neighborhood. Often we disagreed and sometimes the more
we talked, the more we disagreed. We were critical and skep-
tical at times—no one was politely dishonest enough to let a
point pass that called for a challenge. But a generosity of
spirit prevailed in the circle. Talking about the issues exposed
our differences, but it also brought closer together people who
had been strangers when they met. Sometimes we discovered
that, despite our differences, we shared our deepest values
with people who seemed most unlike us. We were constantly
reminded that differences between faiths are real, not to be
papered over for nicety's sake, but we discovered that people
with deep, intractable differences can teach and learn from
each other. When you "listen to the loves of others," as
Thomas Green puts it, minds, hearts, and lives can be profoundly touched with genuine understanding. And we can
begin to grasp what Emerson meant when he said, "We measure all religions by their civilizing power."

IV

So here we are, you and I, not only between two centuries
but between two millennia, facing what the scholar James
Davison Hunter describes as the never-ending work of democracy. It's the tedious, hard, perplexing, messy, and seemingly endless task of working through what kind of people
we're going to be and what kind of communities we will live
in. Religion has to be a part of that conversation—religion as
a wellspring of values reflecting different aspirations for our
moral and political order—religion as the exercise of free men
and women trying to find meaning in the vast universe
around us—religion as the interpretation of life itself.

But how, in the real world of democracy, can I hold my
religious truth to be THE truth when everyone else sees truth
differently? I put this question not long ago to the renowned
scholar of comparative religion, Huston Smith, a wise man
who has spent the whole of his adult life trying to penetrate
the essence of the world's great religions. If you saw that series, you saw Huston Smith actually thinking before he answered—one of those eloquent moments of silence rare on

television—and then he said: "We listen. We listen as alertly to the other person's description of reality as we hope they listen to us. *We listen.*"

This frightens some people. They fear that hearing what others have to say about faith will lead to the loss of their own distinctive tradition. They fear they may have to shed the uniqueness of their own beliefs to embrace a flimsy ecumenism in which all religions are reduced to saying the same thing. They even imagine they'll be dragged into a movement that seeks "one faith for one world."

That hasn't been my experience. To the contrary, I believe myself a more mature Christian—even a better Baptist—for having come to see that all the great religions grapple with things that matter, although each may come out at a different place; that each arises from within and expresses a lived human experience; and that each and every one of them deserves attention for the wisdom they might offer to humanity. Buddhists have taught me about contemplation and the "the infinite within." From Muslims I have learned about the beauty of sobriety and surrender; from Jews about the imperative of justice in a moral order; from Hindus about a universe charged with divinity, and "realms of gold hidden in the depth of our hearts"; from Confucionists about the quality of empathy that supports the fragile web of civilization. Nothing I take from them has come at the expense of confidence in my own story—the Christian story. But I must confess there's something liberating about no longer being quite so tone deaf to what others have to report from their experience of transcendence.

Situated as we are in circumstances particular to our time and place, we humans construct different worldviews from our different angles on reality. It can be wondrous to discover how the same world all of us inhabit appears in different forms through a kaleidoscope of perspectives. Sometimes I think this must be the way God sees the world, too, through the eyes of infinite numbers of creation's children. If so, to transcend the visible spectrum of feeling—to see what others see—we don't have to give up our own faith. We just have to get closer to its source, to God. At least that's the notion I'm struggling with, in a world that looks less and less like me every day.

My friend Nasr has been helpful on this. You saw him in the series. A Moslem scholar of world distinction, and himself a pilgrim into the mysteries of Sufi mysticism, Seyyed

Hossein Nasr is University Professor of Islamic Studies at George Washington University. No one I've listened to recently more lucidly explains the microcosm of the whole globe that has been created within America during the past half century—from wave upon wave of immigration, from the coming and jostling of many dynamic cultures, traditions, beliefs, and aspirations. It is a discombobulating experience, to be sure—like riding a crowded bus on a bumpy ride, and, says Nasr, it tests our mettle. The temptation is that religion gets reduced to the least common denominator, a melange of superficial and borrowed opinions that lead to relativism and even nihilism, where everybody believes everything and yet no one believes anything.

But there is another way, says Nasr. Suppose you hold with conviction to your center, the reality of your experience, and I to mine, but we recognize that each of our faiths is as concerned as the other with the meaning of human life, with the significance of the good in human action, and with the possibility of a transcendent dimension to our earthly existence. Suppose we acknowledge that while someone belonging to another tradition with her own spiritual centers is not "one of us," she is nevertheless one of God's. The writer Kathleen Norris acknowledges in one of her poems that "We are all God's chosen now." But in the next breath she prays, "God help us because we are." The call, you see, is not to pride; the call is to humility. In the words of the Jewish theologian and activist Abraham Joshua Heschel, "No religion is an island. We are all involved with one another. Spiritual betrayal on the part of one affects the faith of all." So let everyone join in the conversation, and let no one monopolize it. Democracy should then do quite well, thank you, in a world of no center—and many.

Since the series I am often asked to identify my favorite verse in the whole of Genesis. I've decided it's the third verse of the second chapter. There we read: "God gave the seventh day his blessing and he hallowed it, for on it he ceased from all his work that by creating, God had made." I take this to mean creation is not finished. Life on earth is incomplete, dynamic, continuously in renewal. Genesis is just the beginning. The millennium is not the end. What happens now to creation is up to us, every one of us.

****

I heartily recommend these books to anyone wishing to explore the subject of the lecture more profoundly: Richard Erdoes, *AD 1000: Living on the Brink of Apocalypse* (San Francisco: Harper & Row, 1988); James B. Wiggins, *In Praise of Religious Diversity* (New York and London: Routledge, 1996); Richard Kyle, *The Last Days Are Here Again* (Grand Rapids: Baker Books, 1998); and Robert Grudin, *On Dialogue: An Essay in Free Thought* (Boston: Houghton Mifflin Co., 1996).

A Jewish Response

On the Dangers of Romanticizing Jewish Life: A Meditation on Bill Moyers's Ecumenical World

MARC H. ELLIS*

One cannot help but applaud the work of Bill Moyers over the years. He has brought a wealth of culture and sensibility to the medium of television, thereby setting a standard to be aimed at for now and in the future. This is especially true of the subject of religion, which others in his industry have thought to be either private and uninteresting or dogmatic and limited. Probing religious figures for their insights and biography has deepened the discussion of religion in America and assured its place in the tapestry of our culture. One thinks here of such diverse persons and topics that Moyers have covered over the years: from Dorothy Day and Robert Grave, to his most recent series on Genesis.

Much of Moyers's focus originates in his own more provincial background as he recalls in his lecture: a Southern Baptist from a small town in Texas. His own circumstances may in fact have provided the foundation for his eye unto the world, his seemingly boundless curiosity and his ability to listen and search for that which hides behind the pause and the silence. How often the provincial is mistaken for the parochial, as the cosmopolitan may be with openness.

---

*MARC H. ELLIS is University Professor of American and Jewish Studies and Director of the Center for American and Jewish Studies at Baylor University. He has written and lectured extensively on Jewish and Christian affairs, concentrating on the topics of Holocaust, Israel/Palestine, and the future of religious thought. His many books include *Toward a Jewish Theology of Liberation* and *Unholy Alliance: Religion and Atrocity in Our Time*. His latest book, *O' Jerusalem: The Contested Future of the Jewish Covenant*, addresses the future of Jews and Palestinians and the covenant so central to Jewish life and history.

Moyers is wide-eyed and principled. As the world opened to him he was and remains transfixed. In his lecture he eloquently chides religious leaders who seek to turn the clock back or forget the limitations of one's discrete vision.

Diversity is key here and the defense of traditional Baptist life, with its involvement in a strict separationist sensibility coupled with a respect for religious freedom, is palpable in Moyers's address. A world of discourse and principle is under siege and often, to Moyers's chagrin, the warriors on the right are his co-religionists.

Moyers seems to be addressing a world that is on the one hand slipping from his control, and on the other, unavailable to an audience at a Christian university in central Texas. Thus his dismissal of the religious right as untrue to its Baptist and American heritage is framed to a large extent within the context of his discovery of the Jewish world. In opposition to a fundamentalist understanding of Scripture, Moyers explains to his audience the Jewish understanding of biblical interpretation, *midrash*, which contextualizes biblical stories within Jewish life and practice.

Midrash is clearly Moyers's weapon of choice against those who would close down the biblical text with rote answers. In this way, Moyers is clearly identified as a liberal and identifies with other liberals, including Jewish liberals who are, like him, also religious. Yet hidden in Moyers's text, or perhaps invisible to him, is a romanticization of *midrash* and Jewish life in general. The Christian religious right is the betrayer and ironically, given the history between Christians and Jews and even recent decisions by the Southern Baptist Convention to proselytize Jews, salvation from that path is found within a Jewish sensibility.

Moyers does mention Jewish religiosity in a negative light, especially when it appears to mirror that of the Christian religious right. In this context, he cites Baruch Goldstein and Yigal Amir, both murderers who use religion to legitimate violence. But the overall tone is a deep respect for the liberal Jewish sensibility embodied in *midrash*, paradoxically, just as that tradition is now being separated from the center of Jewish life. Or perhaps more accurately stated, Moyers celebrates the beauty of *midrash* while the center of Jewish life has shifted to the maintenance of political empowerment in America and in Israel. Though much of the Jewish community can no longer be defined as liberal, even the liberal elements within the Jewish life are tainted with a narrative of

Jewish innocence that is contradicted by the way the contemporary Jewish community operates in the world. Probing the most difficult questions of life is important and invigorating, but the question of silence in the face of Palestinian suffering hovers over *midrash* as an accusing image.

If Moyers does not excuse the religious right from the political implications of its interpretations of Scripture, can Jews be held up as exemplars of an open-minded sensibility when for Palestinians this seems a mockery? Genesis is not about Palestine, though more than a few Jews use the Bible to legitimate their exclusive "right" to the Holy Land, but the double standard that Moyers accuses the Christian religious right of employing—hiding behind the Constitution as they deride it—is not wholly dissimilar to a Jewish framework of biblical interpretation that operates as if the Jewish community is free of a double standard with regard to its own values and expression.

The point here is not to criticize Moyers for failing to address the Christian right and Jewish liberal sensibility as guilty, through deed and silence, of a fundamental hypocrisy, for hypocrisy is available to all and used extensively, especially by those who claim to be religious. Rather the point is to question the depth of Moyers's analysis. Without diminishing his own struggle within Baptist life, Moyers, like all of us, seems to be fighting battles with resources that are diminished or no longer available.

The Jewish world that Moyers entered years ago, one that helped him raise questions in a language and sensibility crucial to his life, is a world that lives on borrowed time. Most of the Jews struggling with the questions that are central to Jewish life, especially the ethical questions of victimization and oppression, have either been forcibly exiled from the Jewish community or have fled it in exasperation. For them *midrash* is a safe haven and protection from the urgent questions of our time and the Holocaust, which often shadows the Genesis series, is likewise a place of refuge. *Midrash* is often used as if nothing has happened since the Holocaust, as if Jews are just emerging from the death camps, and as if Jews, unlike others, cannot do the things that Jews have in fact done.

Moyers's lecture fails here because the difference between a closed and open system is more complex than the comparison he draws between the Christian religious right and the moderate/liberal *midrashic* system. Both a literalist view of the Bible and a *midrashic* interpretative system can be used to deflect questions that confront a contemporary community. Hypocrisy is found everywhere, even with those with whom solidarity is a comfort and a strength. At the same time, important perspectives may be found on all sides, even from those on the other side of the struggle. The elevation of differing perspectives to ontological truths from which a struggle unto death is mandated can reproduce the very cycle Moyers laments.

The changing religious landscape and the power of configurations that loom on the horizon, the very hypocrisy that invades or hovers on the edge of all religious discourse, serve as warnings against unreflective piety. No doubt Moyers would agree with this. Still the question remains as how to proceed. If the world Moyers entered and benefited from—and through him and the medium of television benefited millions—is now coming to a close, the issues remain. Is religion in the new millennium to be a closed system or an open one, seeing its primary task as defining one's salvation or inviting others on a journey whose destination is uncharted or at least not defined in advance? Who will carry these visions forward and will the differing perspectives be seen in the context of holy war or mutually enriching possibilities?

As a Jew involved in the passionate discussions revolving around the Holocaust, Israel and Palestine, and having traveled the world with Christians of different denominations and perspectives, including those who are adherents to liberation theology and those who are committed evangelicals, I can affirm that the future of religion and religiosity is a complex field to work through. On the ecumenical front, it seems a new sensibility is emerging that Moyers alludes to but has not experienced in its coming form: the link between Jews and Christians along their propensity for orthodox or liberal belief and the split within religions and denominations along these same fault lines. In other words, more and more orthodox and liberal believers across religious lines feel closer to one another than to their co-religionists who see faith in a different framework. Here the content of belief is less important than the form it takes: tradition held high is the watchword for the orthodox of all faiths; an open interpretation is the watchword for liberals. Buried are the old controversies about the sufficiency or heresy of Jewish and Christian belief or even the distinctions between them. In this struggle of conservative and liberal a new struggle has been joined, one that is as important as previous struggles.

But there is yet another ecumenism forming beneath and around this more public and institutionalized war. There are Jews and Christians who are no longer within the denominational framework at all or holding at the fringes. Neither the conservative nor liberal sensitivity speak to them or to the people from many countries and other religions with whom they come into contact. Most of these people exist outside organized religion and outside the public discussion of religion as recognized by society. Moreover, many of these people are exiles from their faith communities even as they search out a spirituality and a politics that makes sense of the world in which they live. Strangers to one another, yet sharing similar experiences and perspectives, these exiles are less "other" to one another than they share a common journey. One sees among these exiles a new diaspora forming in our time, a diaspora that will form values and symbols to express its sensibilities and hopes. This diaspora is founded on an ecumenism that is eclectic, with boundary crossing being central to its emerging self-definition.

Too often the weapons of choice in the ongoing struggle surrounding issues of identity and religious practice are forms of religiosity that are passing from the scene or proclaim distinctiveness even as they practice assimilation. The danger is twofold: to embrace what is increasingly empty of substance and to miss the new possibilities forming in our time. Yet a certain respectability is assured if the former is chosen as the frame of reference and the latter remains invisible. Perhaps this is simply generational and we must await the next Bill Moyers for the twenty-first century. Awaiting articulation and broadcast is the new ecumenism and diaspora in our time. It is here that we may move beyond the old struggles and engage the issues that confront us as Americans and people of faith.

An Islamicist Response

The Challenge of Pluralism in the Millennium

JOHN ESPOSITO*

When I first decided to study Islam some thirty years ago, friends and family wondered why. Why study a "foreign" religion; as one colleague said, "an abra kadabra field with no job possibilities." If some saw Hinduism and Buddhism as religions of meditation, enlightenment, and gurus, Islam elicited images of holy war, harems, and oil sheiks.

Raised Roman Catholic in an Italian neighborhood in Brooklyn, an assistant professor of theology in the late 1960s, ignorant of Islam and filled with stereotypes of Arabs, I too had seen no reason to study Islam. However, in order to earn a doctorate at Temple University, we were required to study other faiths regardless of our major. I had studied Hinduism and Buddhism but that was resistant to the strong suggestion by the department chair (a Jewish scholar) that I study Islam with our new Muslim professor, Ismail R. Faruqi.

Imagine my surprise to discover that Islam was indeed a major monotheistic faith with a rich, creative, and dynamic history—a path for hundreds of millions of believers (today 1.2 billion) from North Africa to Southeast Asia and a faith that had informed vast empires and civilizations. Alongside Judaism and Christianity, Hebrew Bible and New Testament, I now discovered Islam and the Quran. When studying about

*JOHN ESPOSITO is the Founding Director of the Center for Muslim-Christian Understanding and a Professor of Religion and International Affairs and of Islamic Studies at Georgetown University. He has served as President of the American Council for the Study of Islamic Societies and as a consultant to the Department of State as well as corporations, universities, and organizations worldwide. Esposito specializes in Islam, political Islam, and the impact of Islamic movements from North Africa to Southeast Asia. He is Editor-in-Chief of *The Oxford Encyclopedia of the Modern Islamic World* and *The Oxford History of Islam*. Among his many other publications are *Islam: The Straight Path, The Islamic Threat: Myth or Reality?*, and *Political Islam: Revolution, Radicalism, or Reform?*

God (One, Just and Compassionate), revelation, prophets, ethical monotheism, social justice, why had no one told me about Islam, of Islam's affinity with Judaism and Christianity? Why was Islam not seen as part of a Judeo-Christian-Islamic monotheistic tradition but instead grouped with Hinduism, Buddhism, and Confucianism? How could I have earned a liberal arts degree with lots of philosophy, history, and religion and known so little about the treasures of Islamic civilization and their contributions to philosophy, mathematics, geometry, medicine, the sciences, arts, and architecture? I soon discovered that the little I had learned about Islam and Muslim-Christian relations was one-sided or distorted, from Dante's Inferno (where Muhammad is consigned to the depths of the inferno) to the victims and the victors of the Crusades to European colonialism and "the white man's burden." Islam had been as invisible and insignificant a reality in American education as Muslims were on the religious landscape. International politics and domestic demographics have led to an explosion of knowledge and coverage about Islam and to a rapidly changing American and Europe where, as Bill Moyers points out, Islam is, respectively, the third and second largest religion. How will our understanding of other religions affect the twenty-first century? Will it be a century of globalization and dialogue or confrontation and conflict?

The impact of modernity and development on religion in the twentieth century proved both constructive and destructive. Reformers and traditionists debated issues of religion's reinterpretation and reform while others declared the irrelevance or end of religion. By the mid-twentieth century, some theologians declared the death of God and the triumph of the "secular city," chronicled by Harvey Cox. At the same time, Western secular presuppositions of modernization theory led many experts to ignore or dismiss the presence and relevance of religion in development, failing to appreciate or foresee its enduring significance in both modern and modernizing societies.

However, in the last decades of the twentieth century the error of such presumption has become clear as the presence and power of religion has reemerged, signaling a global religious resurgence. The resurgence has demonstrated the enduring power of religion and its critique of modernity. Religion has been reasserted not only as a source of identity, meaning, and spiritual sustenance but also as a source of ideology and mass mobilization. It has been used to legitimate liberation as well as oppression. Religion has often been linked to new forms of nationalism and ethnic tribalism, shattering or threatening the existence of nation-states. Its ravages have been seen in Bosnia, Kosovo, Rwanda, Lebanon, India, Sri Lanka, Pakistan, and Indonesia.

Bill Moyers has correctly identified the diverse messianic and apocalyptic voices and forces that exist today. Religious conflicts are difficult to assess, often entailing the need to distinguish secular from religious authoritarian regimes, to differentiate between moderate and extremist (non-violent and violent) religious political opposition or state-initiated violence versus the violence resulting from extremist religious movements. Similarly it is important to distinguish between religious conflicts and communal/sectarian conflicts, that is, between those conflicts whose primary cause is religious as opposed to those that are political and socioeconomic in origin.

Another challenge in the new millennium will be how to understand and assess the global resurgence of religion(s) in politics. As we have seen in twentieth-century conflicts in Northern Ireland, South Africa, Lebanon, India, Kashmir, Nicaragua, and Israel/Palestine, determining the role of religion in political and revolutionary struggles is complex and filled with pitfalls. Our lack of knowledge of Islam coupled with world events have resulted in Islam's continuing to be one of the most misunderstood religions. Bill Moyers's characterization of Afghanistan as a civil war between Sunni and Shii Muslims and of the Algerian civil war as caused primarily by fundamentalist extremists illustrates this point. The Afghan war has not been primarily a rivalry between Sunni and Shii Muslims. It has been a civil war in which Afghan tribal differences and rivalries have been more important than a Sunni-Shii sectarianism. Indeed the overwhelming majority of mujahidin militias throughout the past decade have been Sunni, first fighting Soviet occupation and then warring among themselves. Sunni-Shii cleavages and rivalry, though important, have been secondary.

Similarly, the Algerian civil war is more than simply a battle between a legitimate government and "fundamentalists" who want to impose an Islamic theocracy. In the late 1980s, Algeria, as many other Arab governments, opened up its political system in response to public outrage at failed economies. Algeria, a military-backed one-party system, held its first elections (municipal followed by parliamentary) since gaining independence. In 1991 the Algerian military intervened, in effect seized power, and canceled the results of democratically held elections in which the Islamic Salvation Front (an Islamic movement) had first swept municipal elections and then, having again swept the first round of parliamentary elections, seemed poised to come to power. The heavy-handed response of the military (mass arrests and repression) created conditions that led to a spiral of violence and counter-violence. The resulting polarization and radicalization have devastated Algeria and led to a civil war in which both elements in the military (eradicateurs) and religious extremists (in particular the Armed Islamic Group) have been guilty of violence and savagery.

Our understanding of the changing international as well as domestic roles of religion have both been affected by a European secular bias. Bill Moyers is quite correct when he talks about the extent to which white Protestant males of a culturally conservative European heritage have influenced our understanding of religion. It is equally important to recognize the extent to which a "secular fundamentalist" worldview, heavily indebted to the social sciences, has inhibited our ability to see and assess the role of religion in public life, in politics and society. By "secular fundamentalism," I mean the tendency to believe not that liberal secularism is one of many lenses through which we can see the world and order society but that it is the norm, an imperative rather than an alternative, for every developed and developing society. From a secular fundamentalist point of view the reassertion of religion in public life is automatically seen as a threat. Having underestimated or dismissed the significance of religion, some now risk seeing its reassertion in politics and public life as necessarily irrational or extremist.

As Moyers notes, Christians, Jews, and Muslims increasingly live side-by-side in Europe and America. Our religious landscape has changed dramatically in a matter of decades. If Islam was invisible only two decades ago, our cities and towns across the United States are now dotted with mosques and Islamic Centers. My parents who live in the New York-New Jersey area have Muslim physicians not because of their son's profession but due to the demographic realities of America: Muslims are US!

Changing demographics and global politics will require, as never before, a religious and civilizational dialogue that redefines the notions of pluralism and tolerance that we have held to be our tradition. It is easy for all to denounce the intolerance of religious fundamentalists who blow up abortion clinics, or the World Trade Center, or who massacre Muslims in a Hebron mosque or in Bosnia. It is more difficult to recognize the more subtle distortions and excesses of liberal secularism. Too often the secularism or laicism (France) of Europe and America can seem less about preserving religious freedom for all and more about promoting or imposing a secular state that is anti-religious, dealing with Islam as an alien religion. Rather than acknowledging Muslims as equal members in the family of Abraham and emphasizing the family resemblance of a Judeo-Christian-Islamic tradition, Muslims are still too often transformed into "the other," to be feared or demonized.

In Britain this phenomenon is referred to as Islamaphobia. In France, multiculturalism has been replaced by an insistence on integration and assimilation. French Muslims are told that they must be secular (laic) Muslims, and in French society young women who wish to wear a headscarf (hejab) are banned from attending school and from employment opportunities. In North America, Muslim citizens have not been free from prejudice and misunderstanding. They have often had to struggle for the right to wear hejabs, to be permitted time-off in the workplace to pray, to have chaplains in the military, and to have their major religious holydays/holidays recognized. While a great deal of headway has been made in recent years, especially in the United States, much more remains to be done.

The discussions of religious leaders and scholars on Moyers's Genesis program underscored a major challenge to all believers in the new millennium: tolerance. Tolerance can no longer be simply the minimalist acceptance of "others'" right to exist. Rather tolerance must be based upon recognizing that "others" are full and equal partners in society. Similarly, Muslim populations in Sudan, Pakistan, Egypt, and Indonesia face the challenge of recognizing the equal status and rights of non-Muslim citizens. Pluralism does not require that we surrender or diminish the fundamental beliefs of our faith and identity. As Bill Moyers perceptively notes, we need to be able to disagree passionately without going for our neighbor's throat. Affirmation of the uniqueness of one's own faith need not result in a self-righteous exclusivist identity or community. The existence of diverse religious and ethnic groups has created a rich mosaic within the fabric of American society.

Jews, Christians, Muslims—all Americans of whatever faith—will be challenged in the new millennium to combine recognition (indeed celebration) of religious differences with an awareness of shared beliefs, values, and interests. Just as we do not think of Judaism and Christianity as foreign religions, we will know we are beginning to really understand when we view other religions as a normal part of the American religious landscape. At the end of a course that I taught some years ago on Islam at Holy Cross, I would introduce the senior military officer in charge of the Army ROTC, a Columbia graduate with an M.A. from Johns Hopkins University, to a stunned group of students. He was Muslim but he looked like us and talked like us! Today the major Muslim communities are not simply Cairo, Damascus, Islamabad, or Kuala Lumpur, but also Paris, New York, London, Bonn, Detroit, Los Angeles, and Washington D.C. My students at Georgetown University are an exciting mix of Muslims and non-Muslims. However, one can not necessarily read the religious scorecard by nationality or accent. Many are not simply Muslims in America; they are American Muslims.

An Evangelical Christian Response

"Genesis and the Millennium" and the Challenge of Pluralism

STANLEY J. GRENZ*

Many social commentators in recent years have noted that the Western world is in the midst of immense change. Some go so far as to suggest that we are experiencing a cultural shift that rivals the transition from the Middle Ages to modernity. Our world is increasingly becoming postmodern in ethos.[1] In "Genesis and the Millennium," Bill Moyers raises one of the central questions that emerges as we seek to negotiate the uncharted waters of the postmodern situation. He asks, How do we "live learned lives of faith and value in a world where all of us must increasingly interact with people who are not like us?" In articulating this question, Moyers puts his finger on one particular aspect of the postmodern context that confronts not only Americans, but Western culture in general, at the beginning of the twenty-first century: We live in a "pluralist" society.

---

*STANLEY J. GRENZ is Pioneer McDonald Professor of Baptist Heritage, Theology, and Ethics at Carey Theological College and Professor of Theology and Ethics at Regent College in Vancouver, British Columbia. He has published twenty books including *Sexual Ethics, Theology for the Community of God*, and *A Primer on Postmodernism*. He has also contributed articles to fifteen other volumes, and has written over a hundred essays and an additional eighty book reviews appearing in journals ranging from *Christianity Today* and *Christian Century* to *Christian Scholars Review* and the *Journal of Ecumenical Studies*.

---

1. See Stanley J. Grenz, *A Primer on Postmodernism* (Grand Rapids: Eerdmans, 1996).

The Shape of the Postmodern Pluralist Context

What does this characterization mean? What is pluralism as a cultural phenomenon? Allow me to offer a response from north of the forty-ninth parallel, for I believe that in certain respects the Canadian context signals the direction in which other Western societies, including the United States, are moving.

In Canada pluralism is not merely a de facto, demographic reality. Instead, under the rubric of "multiculturalism" pluralism is official public policy and marks the "official" self-understanding of Canada as a nation. Let me illustrate: On 11 July 1994 together with thirty-plus others I appeared before the citizenship judge for our "swearing in" ceremony. In a homily crafted for this occasion, the judge outlined for us what lies at the heart of being Canadian. Her answer was simple: Canada means multiculturalism.

Although multiculturalism did not become national policy until the 1960s and 1970s, it is an outworking of the "feeling for space"—space in which people of all nationalities and traditions could settle down alongside one another—that has been a part of the Canadian psyche from the beginning. In Canadian historian H. H. Walsh's words, "imperceptibly Canada changed from a bicultural to a multicultural nation in which variety rather than uniformity is encouraged. Indeed, variety has now become a way of life that stands in sharp contrast to modern nationalism with its emphasis upon homogeneity."[2]

Nevertheless, in the years since multiculturalism was enshrined as national policy the immigrant "face" of Canada has changed dramatically. Prior to 1961, 90 percent of immigrants came from Europe. Between 1991 and 1996, in contrast, Europeans accounted for only 19 percent, whereas the percentage of Asian immigrants skyrocketed from a paltry 3 percent to 57 percent. Early in 1999, Michael Adams, author of the best-selling work about life in Canada bearing the intriguing title *Sex in the Snow*, writing in Canada's leading news magazine *Maclean's*, suggested that Canadians change "our 19th century imperialistic motto 'From Sea Even Unto Sea'" to something "more 21st century." His proposal, "Within one,

---

2.   H.H. Walsh, " A Canadian Christian Tradition," in *The Churches and the Canadian Experience: A Faith and Order Study of the Christian Tradition*, ed. John Webster Grant (Toronto: Ryerson Press, 1963), 148.

many,"[3] reflects the Canadian commitment to multiculturalism in keeping with current postmodern sensitivities, while
sounding almost stylistically contrived to stand as a stark contrast to the motto of the United States, "E pluribus unum."

Its multicultural face affects many aspects of Canadian life.
For example, it has reopened the historically unresolved question of the place of First Nations peoples in the Canadian mosaic. More crucial in the context of Moyers's essay, however,
is its effect on the religious climate of the nation. In contrast to
the recent past in which only two main alternatives loomed in
the minds of most people—atheism or Christianity—Canadians find themselves living in a land that embraces many religions and many gods (reminiscent, I might add, of the
situation faced by the early church).

This reality is evident in my home-to-office commute. During the first ten minutes of the thirty-five minute drive, I pass
by, in order, the Hare Krishna temple complete with a huge
statue of Krishna and a vegetarian restaurant, the large church
building that houses a unitarian cult from the Philippines,
several ethnic Chinese churches of various sizes and denominational affiliations, and an imposing Sikh temple. Casting a
slightly wider net would envelop a mosque, a Mennonite
church building that has been converted into a Buddhist temple, and the meeting place of a Wiccan coven.

In the modern era, the original Anglican and Roman Catholic establishments in Canada found themselves needing to
make peace with each other and make room first for "noncon-
formist" Protestants and later for Orthodox churches. In
postmodern Canada, they are coming to terms with religious
traditions from around the world, as well as traditional spiri-
tualities of indigenous peoples. The Canadian experience con-
firms Moyers's conclusion, "we're entering a new religious
landscape in America."

Landmines along the Multicultural Trail

The Canadian experience of multiculturalism, however,
poses issues that lie deeper. There is, of course, the public policy question. In the face of the increasing diversity of its immigrant population and the resurgence of its aboriginal peoples,
will the United States—with its historical preference for the

---

3.   Michael Adams, "Looking for Leadership," *Maclean's* 112/4 (25 Janu-
ary 1999): 53.

image of the melting pot—attempt to remain a nation in the modern sense in accordance with its national motto? Or will it adopt what has been the historic Canadian option—the image of the cultural mosaic? Public policy decisions in the near future will both determine, and be determined by, the answer to this question.

A second issue focuses more directly on the religious identity of the nation. The American religious experience was built on a historic compromise that came to be enshrined in the First Amendment. At the heart of this compromise was "denominationalism," the rejection of a national established church in favor of a multiplicity of churches that were to contribute to the nurturing of public piety. As the nation becomes increasingly multicultural, will the American denominational "establishment" retain its distinctively Christian (or Judeo-Christian) flavor? Or will the United States follow the lead of its northern neighbor, which has witnessed a profound shift from an initial religious establishment to complete religious pluralism?

As Americans ponder their future, the Canadian movement to multicultural pluralism suggests that there are landmines lurking beneath the surface. Of particular interest is the potential danger posed by a cultural relativism born from the multicultural context.

Relativism has become the reigning ethos in multicultural, postmodern Canada. This relativism moves beyond mere tolerance for alien practices and viewpoints to involve the celebration of diversity. At its heart is the assumption that our beliefs and behaviour are functions of our social or cultural context; beliefs are true within the context of the community that espouses them. Therefore, what appears wrong from one vantage point, when viewed from within the community that practices the act, may actually be right.

An episode of *Star Trek: The Next Generation* provides an illuminating illustration. An accident has robbed Lt. Worf of the use of his legs. In Klingon society, this means he is as good as dead. Therefore, in keeping with his own cultural mores, Worf plans to end his life, and he has asked his good friend, Will Riker, to assist him in the death ritual. To Riker, Worf's proposed action constitutes a reprehensible act of suicide. But as the ship captain, Jean-Luc Picard, points out, from Worf's perspective within the context of the Klingon community with its unique set of beliefs, mores, and rituals, what to Riker is immoral is perfectly acceptable.

How should we respond to the religious and moral relativism that seems so endemic to a multicultural society? Many religious conservatives find themselves tempted to "ghettoize" their faith. Believing that they alone possess the truth and wanting to maintain the purity of their beliefs, they retreat into enclaves or supposedly safe havens of religious conformity and uniformity isolated from the wider public forum. Liberals, in contrast, often adopt a "least common denominator" approach that minimizes the differences dividing the diverse religious traditions and focus exclusively on the set of core values and beliefs they supposedly share in common.

In designing the Genesis Project, Moyers rejected both alternatives. The major goal of the program was, in his words, to "show that you can disagree passionately with people about things that matter without surrendering your own principled beliefs." And he reports that in the process, "We were constantly reminded that differences between faiths are real, not to be papered over for nicety's sake, but we discovered that people with deep, intractable differences can teach and learn from each other."

Moyers's sense is correct. Neither alternative provides the way forward in a multicultural world, because neither fosters meaningful and potentially enriching encounters between adherents of differing religious traditions. The former tends to shut down conversation prematurely. The latter, by glossing over their distinctive beliefs, eliminates from view the most interesting aspects of what adherents of differing religious traditions bring to the table.

A Theological Vision for a Pluralist Society

While pointing in the right direction, Moyers's essay stops short. Rather than moving on to develop a theological basis for the new model of religious conversation he supports, Moyers seems to revert back to the liberal "least common denominator" approach he has in practice left behind. Here Moyers appeals to Emerson: "We measure all religions by their civilizing power."

Ultimately, however, this method simply will not provide a transcendent social-religious vision that can foster the kind of mutually-enhancing conversation exemplified in the Genesis Project. Why? There is simply no common "civilizing power" lying behind the various religions, for they espouse differing conceptions as to what constitutes "being civilized."

Nor can we assume some religiously neutral vantage point from which to judge the utility of the different religions. In the end, every least common denominator we claim to have discovered will turn out not to be a universal at all, but merely an expression of a particular religious perspective.

Is there no way beyond cultural relativism? Is there nothing that transcends the multiplicity of social groups and thereby can bring humans from differing communities together into the kind of mutually instructive conversations Moyers advocates? The *Star Trek* episode I mentioned earlier expressed one commonly espoused postmodern response: "friendship." Picard appealed to Riker to remember that he is Worf's friend and thus must do whatever act would be most in accordance with the ideal of friendship. In other words—and this is the insight to which Emerson's statement points—what all communities seek to foster is "community," humans living together in a spirit of neighborliness and friendship. But I must quickly add, cultures differ as to what exactly marks living in this manner.

This observation leads to one crucial aim of the kind of public conversations Moyers's project exemplified. One goal ought to be that of exploring the extent to which the beliefs a religious tradition inculcates in its followers and the practices it fosters actually promote the vision of community that lies at its foundation. In this manner, our discussions as committed devotees of differing religions can assist each in seeing the extent to which we fail to live up to our own stated beliefs and standards.

But the conversation cannot stop here. It must also raise the uncomfortable and "politically incorrect" question of truth. This question takes the form: What transcendent vision of human life lies behind the commitment to conversation itself as the means to mutual enrichment among the conversation partners? Or stated in broader terms, which religious vision carries within itself the foundation for the idea of community that sees the good society as emerging through the contribution of its various members?

Formulated in this manner, our query leads to the Christian vision of community arising as it does out of the biblical narrative and the God of that narrative. Christians speak about a God who is eternally "community," the fellowship of the three trinitarian persons. The Christian vision, in turn, speaks of humankind as "created in God's image," as designed by God to mirror within creation God's own relational character. This Christian vision of God as triune and our purpose as the *imago dei* provides the transcendent basis for the human ideal as persons-in-relationship and human social life as unity-in-diversity. Just as God is a plurality-in-unity or a unity-of-plurality, so also the task of society is to be a unity of the multiplicity of its participants, as is reflected in the motto of the United States. And the human quest for community, wherever it is found, is not misguided, for at its heart it is nothing less than our human quest as the divine image to mirror in the midst of all creation the eternal reality of God.

To be complete, however, the larger national conversation Moyers's project exemplified on a smaller scale requires one additional theological assumption, a theological perspective so courageously articulated by the early Baptists whose legacy Moyers holds dear (as I do). These pioneers of an open and mutually beneficial religious conversation were motivated by a great confidence in the power of truth. As the eighteenth-century Baptist advocate of religious liberty, Isaac Backus, declared so forthrightly in the title of one of his many tracts, "truth is great and will prevail."[4] His optimistic view of truth led Backus to argue passionately for a free and open society, for he believed that "truth certainly would do well enough if she were once left to shift for herself."[5] Imbued with faith in the convincing power of truth, the early Baptists engaged in the public forum. And they established congregations which encouraged the participation of all members in the task of seeking the will of Christ for the church, for they believed that in the midst of the conversation involving diverse voices speaking from their heartfelt convictions, God speaks.

How, then, do we "live learned lives of faith and value in a world where all of us must increasingly interact with people who are not like us?" There are no easy answers to the questions posed by our multicultural context. Yet the resources of the Christian faith point the way forward. Our faith mediates to us a profound vision of God as eternally triune, a unique understanding of ourselves as created to reflect the divine reality and a deep trust in the convincing power of truth. Taken

---

4. Isaac Backus, *Truth is Great and Will Prevail* (Boston, 1781), in *Isaac Backus on Church, State, and Calvinism: Pamphlets, 1754-1789*, ed. William McLoughlin (Cambridge: Harvard University, 1968), 402.
5. Isaac Backus, *A Letter to a Gentleman in the Massachusetts General Assembly, concerning Taxes to support Religious Worship* (printers not given, 1771), 5.

together, these theological commitments provide the basis for a society in which a diversity of voices can enter freely in the conversation. We can be advocates of and participants in such a society, believing that in some way this conversation is a foretaste of the day when "the kings of the earth will bring their glory" into the new Jerusalem (Rev. 21:24 NRSV).

An Orthodox Christian Response

An Orthodox Christian Response to Bill Moyers's "Genesis and the Millennium"

STANLEY S. HARAKAS*

I am grateful for the opportunity to reflect and respond to Mr. Moyers's "Genesis and Millennium" talk, even though I could not help but notice that among many paradoxes in his statement, the Orthodox Church was never mentioned, a religion of about a hundred to a hundred and fifty million adherents. Lest anyone misunderstand from the beginning, I am neither surprised nor affronted. In this part of the world it is "standard operating procedure." We are largely invisible in the media of our own country even though together in all of our various jurisdictions (mostly ethnically based) we come close in numbers to some of the more notable mainline Protestant bodies.

The paradox is increased, because in many ways Orthodox Christians and the major groupings in which they find themselves organized in the United States, essentially try to follow the tolerant, ecumenical, "conversational" speaking and listening, non-confrontational stance that Mr. Moyers advocates in his presentation. For example, the main canonical Orthodox churches, organized in the Standing Conference of Canonical Orthodox Churches of America, participate in the National Council of Churches of Christ in the United States, which

---

*STANLEY S. HARAKAS, a priest of the Greek Orthodox Archdiocese of America under the Ecumenical Patriarchate of Constantinople, is Archbishop Iakovos Professor of Orthodox Theology, Emeritus, Holy Cross Greek Orthodox School of Theology, Brookline, Massachusetts. He has been active in the ecumenical movement on local, state, and international levels. He is the author of twelve books, over 135 scholarly articles, and has written a weekly religious column in a national Greek-American newspaper since 1980 to the present. Rev. and Mrs. Harakas are now retired, living in Spring Hill, Florida.

seeks to foster some of the understanding and conversation Mr. Moyers advocates. The NCCC, too, was not mentioned.

My intent is not to complain. It is to indicate that the ecumenical approach is something which has been tried and in many ways has succeeded in fostering a tolerant, ecumenical, "conversational," speaking and listening, non-confrontational stance. But it is also fragile in many ways and open to failure as a result.

The Merits of Dialogue

In these ecumenical venues, Christian churches of sharply different theologies and ecclesial structures have sought to address their different visions of the Christian way of believing and living for the sake of Christian unity. For some five decades the World Council of Churches, founded in 1948, has fostered the method of listening and understanding among the traditions in ecumenical dialogue. Dialogue requires some of the attitudes present in the Genesis Program conversations, that is, "speaking the truth in love."

Ecumenical dialogue requires that one *speak* honestly, but also courteously and with civility, of one's own faith tradition without compromise and without a proselytizing attitude. Ecumenical dialogue also requires that one *listen* honestly and courteously and with civility and respect and openness to understand the other's position and to learn from it. It is a demanding and difficult enterprise.

My own experience as an educator-scholar priest of the Orthodox Church has brought me into a wide range of dialogues. I have served as a World Council of Churches theological consultant in numerous international ecumenical gatherings, including two World Assemblies of the WCC, and in this country, in Orthodox co-sponsored ecumenical meetings with Jews, Muslims, Roman Catholics, Lutherans, Reformed, and yes, Baptist Christians. In all of these dialogues I have offered written contributions that have been included in the subsequently published proceedings of the meetings.

I have profited from this experience of dialogue in many ways. The most significant gain is that I have learned from the perspectives of other religious traditions with which I have been in dialogue. In particular, I have been led to see and affirm parts of my own Orthodox traditions that have, for historical reasons primarily, been forgotten, submerged, or remained undeveloped. I have been changed, not by adopting views of other religions, but by being led to re-examine the sources of my own Orthodox tradition and discovering there untapped sources that were being ignored or unexploited. The dialogic approach has served not only to help others understand Orthodox experience and theological understandings, but has also dispelled many Orthodox misunderstandings of others. True dialogue is always at least a two-way street.

An example, involving a Baptist minister, that took place in a Roman Catholic Seminary outside Baltimore, occurred in 1980 during a preparatory conference regarding the "Baptism-Eucharist-Ministry" (BEM) document which was adopted by the WCC Faith and Order Commission in Lima, Peru in 1982. I was involved in a small group discussion circle on the third and ecumenically most difficult aspect of the document, "Ministry." The presentations had made clear that the episcopal dimension of ministry was biblical, apostolic, and never absent from the life of the church of the first and subsequent centuries. As *The Dictionary of the Ecumenical Movement* puts it, "the 'episcopal succession' is proposed as a 'sign, though not a guarantee,' of the continuity and unity of the church." The article continues, "the three-fold ministry of the bishop, presbyter and deacon may serve today as an expression of the unity we seek and also as a means for achieving it."

Sitting next to me was an elderly Baptist minister, who listened to the discussion in silence. Toward the end of our session, he bowed his head and moved it back and forth. Misunderstanding the message he was conveying, I asked him, "Aren't you convinced that what BEM says about bishops is true?" He looked at me and with a strained expression on his face, he responded, "Yes, I am convinced." Then resuming his rueful head shaking he asked, "Yes, but what am I going to tell them back home?" Dialogue, you see, has consequences for all who participate in it. I have changed and been deepened in my understanding of my own faith, but also I have entered into the struggle that dialogue provokes for others. In genuine dialogue all involved are enriched.

The Importance of Dialogue

So, dialogue of the kind that Mr. Moyers advocates has been around for fifty long years of mutual information, challenge, and growth. I believe in it. The Orthodox Church has shown that it believes that it is the only proper way to cultivate the spirit of unity. But, unfortunately, it has not tended to work out always as we have hoped. In the judgment of many Orthodox, a subtle change came into the ecumenical world in the last decade. Dialogue began to be replaced by advocacy. The ecumenical movement tended toward abandoning the concern of Christian unity—with its concomitant use of dialogue—and began to replace it with activism seeking to change its member churches' beliefs and in committing them to courses of action in which they had no agreement.

It became, in the judgment of many of its Orthodox member churches, an agency not of the churches, but an instrument for advancing the theological and ethical stances only some of its members held to. As long ago as the Canberra, Australia, 1991 WCC Assembly, the Orthodox felt estranged and began to reconsider their participation in the WCC. The period leading to the 1998 WCC in Harare, Zimbabwe sharpened those feelings. The Patriarchate of Jerusalem had long since ceased any kind of participation in the life and activities of the WCC. By the time of the December Assembly, the Orthodox churches of the nations of Georgia and Bulgaria had announced their withdrawal from the organization. The Orthodox Church of Russia, the largest of the Orthodox churches and the largest single church in the WCC, had decided to curtail its participation in the organization to the minimum. The Orthodox churches were perilously close to withdrawing from the WCC *en masse*. Dialogue had broken down. There was no reason to stay. They spoke, but no one was *listening* to them.

Only the persistent efforts of the Ecumenical Patriarchate of Constantinople stemmed the tide of withdrawal from the WCC, at least for the moment. The Orthodox churches, with a few exceptions, were represented at the Harare Assembly. But finally, the leadership of the ecumenical agency began, once again, *to hear* what they were saying.

So in an article distributed by the Ecumenical Newservice International on the last day of the Assembly, December 14, 1998, Stephen Brown wrote,

One of the most sensitive issues at the assembly has been the question of the relationships between the WCC's Orthodox and non-Orthodox member churches. The assembly voted on December 12 to set up a theological commission to look at possible changes in the "structure, style, and ethos" of the WCC. However, it was also revealed during the assembly that the Bulgarian Orthodox Church had officially withdrawn from the WCC, and that the Russian Orthodox Church was suspending its full participation in the WCC's central committee while the special commission conducts its deliberations.

Konrad Reiser, the head of the WCC, was reported as saying that "The commission would 'look seriously at the questions that have been causing concern to the Orthodox churches for a long time' but to which the WCC 'has not found the right way of responding, at least to the satisfaction of its Orthodox member churches.'" According to Brown, Reiser "added that it had also become clear 'that the concerns of the Orthodox are shared also by other member churches.'"

So maybe "not listening" had become a habit of those in power and authority. But Harare was the place where it was admitted, and some effort was made to work toward re-establishing the dialogue.

Speaking and listening may begin again. Or, of course, it may be too late. NBC News reported recently that Afghanistan's Taliban leaders have opened their closed communication channels to request a resumption of aid and assistance from the United Nations. It is a small crack in the confrontational policies of the Taliban. It is an admission that others may have something that they need to receive. Is it the possible opening of dialogue? Speaking and listening may, indeed, be possible again.

But when so much that is deemed important and essentially non-negotiable is placed on the table, it is not easy. It is not easy to enter into, it is not easy to sustain, it is not easy to tell one's story authentically, but also in a way that allows the other *to hear* us. Above all, it is not easy really, honestly, and empathetically *to listen* to what the dialogue partner is saying.

That is what Mr. Moyers's call to conversation needs so as to give it some realism. For, I think he would agree that it is the only way genuinely open to a world in which weapons serve as the ultimate source of coercion. If we are not in some form of conversation and dialogue, it is the horrendous voice of guns and bombs and rockets, yes, and nuclear weaponry that speak.

On a hill in my home institution, which I served for just short of thirty years as a faculty member and for a third of that time as a dean, there is a statue of that great spokesman of dialogue and advocate of the method of persuasion, Patriarch Athenagoras Spyrou, who died in 1972. He was instrumental in December of 1965 in bringing about the abrogation of the anathemas of 1054 (that's 911 years later!) which contributed to the split of the Roman Catholic and Orthodox churches. Athenagoras worked to enhance Inter-Orthodox unity in which "he proposed [but never imposed] initiatives," according to the French Orthodox scholar Olivier Clement. He encouraged Orthodox participation in the WCC as well as numerous bilateral consultations and dialogues, including one with Islam.

On the base of the statue on the ground of Holy Cross Greek Orthodox School of Theology are written these words in Greek and English: "Elate na koitachthoume"—"Come, let us look into each others' eyes." When we do that, we are relating with real people, not stereotypes, not mental constructs, not propaganda images. Dialogue is possible. But even then it is not easy. When it is difficult, then the temptation to turn one's head and eyes away is very strong. That is when the words "Come, let us look into each others' eyes" are essential. Sharing, listening, hearing, persuasion are the only ways to avoid mutual and perhaps eventual total destruction.

Concluding Thoughts

I close with two very old passages from the early years of the Christian church's history. They can be understood as applying to any kind of important conversation involving fundamental concerns that may lead to modifying or enriching dialogue. However, they speak of the modes of religious relations.

The early Tertullian (160-225) taught in the Western part of the church at a time when the Roman Empire was persecuting Christians: "It is a fundamental human right, a privilege of nature, that every man should worship according to his own convictions. One man's religion neither harms nor helps another man. It is certainly no part of religion to compel religion on another. Free will, and not force, should lead us." (*To Scapula*, ch. 2.)

And that preeminently Eastern Christian Church Father, St. John Chrysostom (347-407), speaking to every person who is convinced of his understanding of the truth, offers counsel worthy of being heeded. He, in speaking of pastoral relations, urges the avoidance of force, affirms engagement, and advocates the means of exposition and persuasion, values applicable to dialogue and conversation: "if a human being wanders away from the right faith, great exertion, perseverance, and patience are required; for he cannot be dragged back by force, nor constrained by fear, but must be led back by persuasion to the truth . . . For it is not possible for any one to cure a man by compulsion against his will." (*On the Priesthood*, Bk. 2, 4.)

Indeed, "Come, let us look into each others' eyes," hard and difficult as that may be.

A Mainline
Christian Response

Framing "Genesis and the Millennium": What is Going on When Bill Moyers Speaks

MARTIN E. MARTY*

The secret is out. Bill Moyers is by vocation first of all a teacher. Northrop Frye in *The Great Code* (Harcourt Brace Jovanovich, 1982, p. xv) portrays one such:

[The teacher] is someone who attempts to re-create the subject in the student's mind, and his strategy in doing this is first of all to get the student to recognize what he already potentially knows, which included breaking up the powers of repression in his mind that keep him from knowing what he knows. That is why it is the teacher, rather than the student, who asks most of the questions.

The secret is out. Bill Moyers set out to fulfill the vocation of the teacher by having become professionally an interviewer. He may produce any number of programs, write any number of books, make any number of speeches, but consistently he is the teacher "who asks most of the questions." Interviewing, as he admits on these pages, is a favored way to frame such an approach to work and life.

The secret is out. Bill Moyers wants to teach us what he has learned as an interviewer, and what he models in his way

---

*MARTIN E. MARTY is Fairfax M. Cone Distinguished Service Professor at the University of Chicago. He directs the Public Religion Project and is senior scholar-in-residence at the Park Ridge Center for Health, Faith, and Ethics. Widely acknowledged as one of America's leading religious historians, his many honors include the National Book Award and the Medal of the American Academy of Arts and Sciences. Among his most recent works is the multi-volume *Modern American Religion*.

of living: to be conversers. Conversation is his main mode of pursuing truth, and he invites us to join in the pursuit. Students of the science and art of conversing consistently point out the difference between argument and conversation.

If Mr. Moyers were arguing, he would lead off by stating a truth that he is ready to defend, an argument that is the end and the beginning of whatever discourse follows. Arguers do research or dip into their own prejudices, line up all the rhetorical armament they can muster, and fire away. While the arguer speaks, he is king of the hill, and you must defend yourself or counterattack by fighting uphill. He will either threaten you until, still not really convinced, you find reason to join him in defending hill-country truth, or he will bash you as you climb, or drive you away.

The converser, however, begins not with the answer but with the question or questions. Note that I did not say "begins and ends," since conversation is never-ending. There is no king of the hill, and there is not even a hill. The participants are on the same plane or the same plain, though they may bring different experiences, different areas of expertise, and different vantages to the engagement. No one leaves saying, "I won *that* conversation." More likely those who took part say something like "I learned something from that conversation." Moyers claims thus to learn ["Conversation is the art of hearing as well as being heard"]. I will not argue with him—though I will look forward to our next conversation.

So much for framing. Do you get the picture? He is trying to do what Frye says a teacher first does. He "attempts to re-create the subject in the student's mind." Moyers's announced subject is Genesis and the Millennium, the beginning and the ending of what we now are and know and have. So let's follow up on his subject. Moyers is "re-creating" because he knows that everyone in front of him or everyone reading him now, does think about beginnings and ends. These have to do variously with the self, the culture, the nation, the civilization, the world and, one supposes, at least now and then, of the universe. But we students deal with all of them in diffuse and random ways until the teacher comes to re-create the subject and focus it in our minds.

Second, says Frye, the teacher's "strategy in doing this is first of all to get the student to recognize what [she] already potentially knows." Here is where Bill Moyers is a bit tricky. Between "Genesis . . . ." and "Millennium" are the words "and the." Moyers is here connecting the beginning "and the" end.

He knows, we know, that the vast majority of our time and energy goes into living in the between, in ordinary minutes or epochs between the first word and the last word. Now we have to listen closely to learn what it is that he is *really* getting at.

The student "already knows" the basic stories of Genesis. Moyers assumes that we can key into "Moses" and "Sarah," into stories of strange people who use the Bible to project weird predictions about the end. How long our culture can take any of these for granted is another question, for another day. Moyers assumes that at least at Baylor some in his audience have a bit of a corner of a reminiscence of a text that tells of such people and such ends. But there is something else we *don't* know, and it is this that makes what we "already potentially know" significant.

Here is what I hear Moyers leading up to by telling the story of how he came to produce a series on Genesis using the set of people he selected to converse on television. While "we" potentially know our own particular story of beginnings and ends, we now inhabit a world where there are many *different* stories. For some today, the main accounts are scientific, stressing as they do the Big Bang beginning and supertitanic "whoosh-sound" of everything getting sucked into blackness or nothingness somewhere in the future, and the end. For some Native Americans the account may be tribal and mythic. The origins of everyone and everything is at *sipapu*, a crevice in the earth such as the Grand Canyon. The destiny of everyone is to leave this world and be with the Great Spirit. In Moyers's reading, Buddhists and Hindus, Muslims and New Agers, all have different readings. We "potentially know that," if we read statistics or use our eyes and watch who is waiting on the steps for the newest moving van in our neighborhood and watching people disembark to live next door, people who are *not* like us.

Moyers also knows, as his lines about how religion "kills" as well as it "heals" show, that his knowledge of diversity, manyness, pluralism, heterogeneity, otherness, and difference, is something we may not naturally want to recognize. Americans have been known on occasion to enslave the other, reservate others or say "dammit, there goes the neighborhood" when someone different moves in. In Frye's term, slightly paraphrased, this means "breaking up the powers of repression in our minds that keep us from knowing what we know." Some of Moyers's breaking up breaks us up; there's a sly humor here that is subversive of pretentious arguers and overstated argument. But it keeps the conversation going. No one is defeated, even if all are at first only half-convinced. The powers of repression do not yield easily.

So we come to the final line of Northrop Frye, ending where we begin, with the teacher. When all is done and said, Moyers remains the teacher who, "rather than the student, . . . asks most of the questions." In this case the question is: what are you going to do with the pluralism you know is inescapable? What are you going to do with the other, the different one, who shares humanity but not all the specifics of *your* and your people's story?

Have I cheated or distorted Moyers's words by saying that this is an essay not so much on "Genesis" and the "Millennium" as with what goes on in the "and the" times? It is true that this is a conversational incentive to keep us conversing so that we listen better, rather than a story about the making of *Genesis* for television. How does it avoid being a moralizing and clubbing of our brains with counsel and demands that we understand "the other" and difference? It is more and other than all of the above.

What I hear in Moyers, the homecoming Baptist, coming home to whatever was Baptist in his beginning and drawing on what will be such at his end, whatever his philosophy, way of life, or religious registration may be by then, is this: one can overcome repression and take risks of overcoming repression for a reason. That reason has to do with the implicit witness to God that runs through Moyers and his midrashim. He tantalizes us to make up stories that help us recreate the possibilities that are before us in the "and the" between times.

Oh, one more thing demands notice: the *where* of this talk that becomes a bid for conversation. This is Bill Moyers, always conscious of place, returning home to a place that had not literally been home: Baylor. No doubt had he given a talk like this in *partibus infidelium*, the country of infidels, for example, in an ancient prestigious university in, say, the northeast of Texans' fantasy that is the godless corner of the country—Moyers may have assumed less knowledge about Genesis than he did at Baylor. He may have had to start from scratch. In such a setting he might well have dealt with the triumph of relativism among people who are all too conscious of diversity and pluralism. Here he was "home," in the country of Baptists and their kin, re-creating, strategizing, breaking up repressions, and asking the questions. He seems to be reassuring his listeners that relativism is not the necessary corollary of pluralism—that one can be conscious of "the other" and other ways of speaking about God, Genesis, "and the," and the millennium and not lose one's roots, not be deprived of every kind of truth.

His is no pontifical pronouncement, no self-assured proclamation of faith. Instead, it is the teacher's quiet questioning witness that does not turn us away, agree with him or not; it impels us to draw our chairs closer. Closer to the desk where stories about Genesis and the Millennium await exploration, closer to the teacher who teases conversation out of us, and, in a world where closeness often issues in tribal warfare, closer to our fellow listeners and conversers.

And that's no secret.

A Mormon Response

A New Millennium, A New Religious Landscape

ROBERT L. MILLET*

I am pleased to be asked to participate in this important conversation. I found Bill Moyers's address, "Genesis and the Millennium," to be stimulating and provocative. I will comment briefly on the religious buzz that is taking place at the start of a new millennium and then speak more extensively on the need for greater breadth and openness in religious dialogue.

I

Eschatology, or the study of "end times," is an important dimension of life and theology of members of The Church of Jesus Christ of Latter-day Saints. What the Latter-day Saints believe about the events to come impacts significantly how they now live and conduct themselves. Without a knowledge of what lies ahead, one cannot have the proper perspective of the overall plan of God to save his children. LDS scriptures are thus filled with references to the last days, to both great and dreadful things that lie ahead. A knowledge of the glories and the trials does much to motivate individuals and congregations to greater fidelity and devotion, to "hold on" to the iron rod, the word of God. The growing fascination in today's world with such phenomena as the Near Death Experience, angels, miracles, etc., attests to men and women's deepest desires to make sense out of what would otherwise be a chaotic existence, a yearning to know that there is a God,

---

*ROBERT L. MILLET is Dean of Religious Education and Professor of Ancient Scripture at Brigham Young University. He received his bachelor's and master's degrees from BYU in Psychology and his Ph.D. from Florida State University in Religious Studies and Psychology. He joined the BYU faculty in 1983. Professor Millet is the author or editor of over thirty books and ninety articles dealing mostly with the history and doctrine of the LDS Church.

that there is life after death, that there is purpose to some of the ironies and challenges of today's world.

Latter-day Saints believe that God can and does speak to men and women through inspiration. They believe the Almighty can make his will known for the world through prophets, and that those prophets have the capacity not only to speak for the present but also to predict future occurrences. The LDS therefore accept wholeheartedly the predictive prophecies in the scriptures. LDS church leaders have counseled the members of the church to take a wholesome and sane approach to prophecy, to study and be aware of the prophetic word but to live each day with confidence and conviction that God is in his heaven and will bring to pass his purposes in the process of time. Church leaders have therefore counseled against what might be called either eschatomania (an unhealthy obsession with signs of the times) and eschatophobia (an unhealthy fear of what lies ahead).

Mormons have been counseled for decades to prepare for what lies ahead, and each family has been encouraged to work toward having a year's supply of food and fuel, as well as a moderate amount of money in savings. Although there are always those who tend to react and overreact to such counsel through doomsday living, by crying out that "The sky is falling"—those who are caught up in PMT, the premillennial tension that Moyers mentioned—Latter-day Saints have been encouraged to engage in provident living, to take the future seriously but to live in the world. In that sense, the Y2K problem, coupled with the millennial fervor in the air, have stirred a few Mormon imaginations, but church leaders continue to advise against rumor, speculation, and in general the kind of frenzied attitudes that both evidence and perpetuate emotional and spiritual instability. In short, we try not to take counsel from our fears.

As Christians, Latter-day Saints do believe in Jesus Christ—in his divinity, his teachings, his miracles, and his death and bodily resurrection. We also believe that He will come again in glory to reign as King of kings and Lord of lords. That is, we believe in the Second Coming of Christ: that it is a fixed time, and that we are obviously closer to that great or dreadful day than were the people who lived in the first century. The very name of the church, The Church of Jesus Christ of Latter-day Saints, epitomizes our belief that these are in fact the last days. We do not, however, believe that the Second Coming will take place right away or that our preparations for that day should be any different than if it were five hundred years from now. As Jesus pointed out in the Parable of the Ten Virgins, there are some things—like years of personal devotion and meaningful service—that one cannot borrow from a neighbor on the spur of the moment. Reservoirs of faith and spiritual depth must be built gradually. We believe that the way to peace and preparation is not through spiritual marathons at the last hour, but rather through consistent and steady spiritual progress throughout our lives. Those who are prepared need not fear.

II

I was touched by Bill Moyers's invitation for the people of the world, especially those in America, to stop talking and listen a little more often and a little more carefully, particularly to those who are different from us. There are simply too many people out there who feel deeply about the vital place of religion in their life, whose spiritual roots run deep, for us to surrender the conversation about public policy and morality and decency and ethics to those who want to trivialize and thereby marginalize religion. On the other hand, the last thing we need is for good men and women to squabble over their differences, to engage in name-calling and misrepresentation, ostensibly in an effort to be true to one's religious persuasion. Such things do little to enhance one's own position; rather, they tend to dilute our strength and skew those efforts that could be directed toward the problems of our day. There *is* a crying need for listening ears and inquiring minds, for people to stretch themselves and climb out of their comfort zone.

Few things are needed more in this complex world than understanding. Unfortunately, religious discussions too often devolve into wars of words as a result of defensiveness over this or that theological issue. On the other hand, I have been involved in some truly remarkable conversations during the last several years, sharing and comparing and contrasting the vexations of the soul that took place between people who honestly wanted to know about the other person's faith and way of life. I am persuaded that religious dialogue is vital if we are to come to that understanding out of which we can derive meaningful engagement of the pressing problems that face us as we begin the twenty-first century.

About two years ago one of my colleagues and I were contacted by the LDS Church Public Affairs Office and asked if we would be willing to participate in an interview with representatives of another Christian faith. We were informed that they were preparing a video presentation on The Church of Jesus Christ of Latter-day Saints, in an effort to better inform members of their own church. Our interview lasted for about an hour and a half. We covered much ground, including the LDS view of prophets, our views concerning the Bible, the person and nature of God, and our teachings on Jesus Christ. For at least twenty or thirty minutes I described our understanding of the Atonement and of the necessity of the mercy and grace of Christ. When their video was released about a year later, I felt that it portrayed quite accurately, for the most part, our fundamental beliefs and, of course, the differences between Latter-day Saints and other religious groups. One aspect was, however, particularly troublesome to me: the narrator stated over and over that the Latter-day Saints are not Christian and thus do not believe in the grace of Jesus Christ.

Several months later, my colleague and I were invited to meet once again with representatives of this other faith. They were eager to know our feelings about the movie. We commented that it was nice that Mormons had been allowed to express themselves. But I also voiced my disappointment in what was said about our lack of belief in Christ and thus in grace. I said, essentially, "If you want to say that the Latter-day Saints have an *unusual* view of grace, or a *deficient* view of grace, or a *false* view of grace, we can live with that, for we obviously differ on the matter of the delicate balance between grace and works. But to say that we have *no* view of grace is a serious misrepresentation that confuses and misleads people."

This episode highlights what I believe to be an important issue in meaningful dialogue: people ought to be allowed to express their views, and we ought to believe them. We don't have to agree with their beliefs, but it accomplishes precious little to ask a person what he believes and then to ignore his observations or to respond, as the interviewer did to me (at least five times), "Yes, but you don't *really* believe that." After hearing that phrase repeatedly, I said: "You know, I don't mean to be defensive or unkind, but I'm an expert on what I believe. I have no reason to be dishonest with you."

Two or three years ago, another colleague and I traveled with two Evangelical Christian friends to another part of the country to meet with a well-known theologian, author, and pastor/teacher in that area. We had read several of his books and had enjoyed his preaching over the years. As a part of an outreach effort to better understand those of other faiths (and to assist them to understand us a little better), we have visited such institutions as Notre Dame, Catholic University, Wheaton College, and various religious colleges and seminaries. We met this particular pastor and then attended his church service on both Sunday morning and Sunday evening, and in both meetings were impressed with the depth and inspiration of his preaching.

The next day we met for lunch and had a wonderful two-hour doctrinal discussion. I explained that we had no set agenda and were not exactly sure why we had chosen to come to California, except that we had admired his writings and wanted to meet him. We added that we had several questions we wanted to pose in order to better understand Evangelical theology. I mentioned that I oversaw the teaching of religion of some 30,000 young people at Brigham Young University and that I felt it would be wise for me to able to articulate properly the beliefs of our brothers and sisters of other faiths. I hoped, as well, that they might make the effort to understand our beliefs so as to represent accurately what we teach.

Early in our conversation the minister said something like, "Look, anyone knows there are big differences between us. But I don't want to focus on those differences. Let's talk about Christ." We then discussed the person of Jesus, justification by faith, baptism, sanctification, salvation, heaven, hell, agency and predestination, premortal existence, and a number of other fascinating topics. We compared and contrasted, we asked questions, and we answered questions. In thinking back on what proved to be one of the most stimulating and worthwhile learning experiences of our lives, the one thing that characterized our discussion, and the one thing that made the biggest difference, was the mood that existed there—a mood of openness, candor, and a general lack of defensiveness. We knew what we believed, and we were all committed to our own religious tradition. But we were eager to learn where the other person was coming from.

This experience says something to me about what can happen when men and women of good will come together in an attitude of openness and in a sincere effort to better understand and be understood. During the last year, a third colleague and I visited Wheaton College in Illinois on two different occasions. The first trip was simply an opportunity

to get to know some of the religion faculty there, to visit religion and history classes, and to become acquainted with the
personnel and resources at the Marion E. Wade Center, which
houses the largest collection of C.S. Lewis materials in the
world. We learned of an upcoming conference on Lewis and
requested information. A call for papers was sent to me, and I
made a proposal. The organizing committee accepted my
proposal and explained that they would be delighted to have
me come.

My paper provided an LDS perspective on the theology of
C.S. Lewis, dealing mostly with why Lewis's thinking is so
well received among the Mormons. We had an unforgettable
experience there and came away richly blessed for the association, the conversations, and the exchange. Again, everyone
there, faculty and students alike, knew of our religious differences, but no one seemed eager (at least in the public settings)
to label us as cultists or to suggest that we had some malicious
purpose or ulterior motive for being there. The questions
from students and faculty were courteous, thoughtful, and
contributive to meaningful dialogue.

Given the challenges we face in our society—fatherless
homes, child and spouse abuse, divorce, poverty, spreading
crime and delinquency, spiritual wickedness in high places—
it seems so foolish for men and women who believe in God,
whose hearts and lives have been surrendered to that God, to
allow doctrinal differences to prevent them from working together. Okay, you believe in a triune God, that the Almighty
is a spirit, and that he created all things *ex nihilo*. I believe that
God is an exalted Man, that he is a separate and distinct per-
sonage from the Son and the Holy Ghost. He believes in
heaven, while she believes in Nirvana. She believes that the
Sabbath should be observed on Saturday, while her neighbor
feels that the day of corporate worship should be on Friday.
This one speaks in tongues, that one spends much of his time
leading marches against social injustice, while a third believes
that little children should be baptized. One good Baptist is a
strict Calvinist, while another tends to take freedom of the
will quite seriously. And so on, and so on.

Latter-day Saints do not believe that the answer to the
world's problems is ultimately to be found in more extrava-
gant social programs or stronger legislation. Most all of these
ills have moral or spiritual roots. In the spirit of the brother-
hood and sisterhood of humankind, is it not possible to lay
aside theological differences long enough to address the stag-

gering social issues in our troubled world? My recent interactions with men and women of various faiths have had a profound impact on me; they have broadened my horizons dramatically and reminded me—a sobering reminder we all need once in a while—that we are all sons and daughters of the same Eternal Father. We may never resolve our differences on the Godhead or the Trinity, or the spiritual or corporeal nature of Deity, or on the sufficiency or inerrancy of the Bible, but we can agree that there is a God; that the ultimate transformation of society will come only through the application of moral and religious solutions to pressing issues; and that the regeneration of individual hearts and souls is foundational to the restoration of virtue in our communities and nations. One need not surrender cherished religious values or doctrines in order to be a better neighbor, a more caring citizen, a more involved municipal.

In addition, we can have lively and provocative discussions on our differences, and such interactions need not be threatening, offensive, or damaging to our relationships. What we cannot afford to do, if we are to communicate and cooperate, is to misrepresent one another or ascribe ulterior motives. Such measures are divisive, and do not partake of that Spirit that strengthens, binds, and reinforces. LDS Church President Gordon B. Hinckley said of the Latter-day Saints: "We want to be good neighbors; we want to be good friends. We feel we can differ theologically with people without being disagreeable in any sense. We hope they feel the same way toward us. We have many friends and associations with people who are not of our faith, with whom we deal constantly, and we have a wonderful relationship. It disturbs me when I hear about any antagonisms. . . . I don't think they are necessary. I hope we can overcome them."

I would take issue, to some degree, with Professor Elaine Pagels's statement, cited in Moyers's address, that "There's practically no religion I know of that sees other people in a way that affirms that other's choice." Latter-day Saints take a rather unusual stand on the matter. We claim to be a restoration of primitive Christianity and thus claim to possess the saving truths and the divine power to act in the name of God. At the same time, we are very much aware of the fact that the Almighty is moving in mysterious ways to spread light and truth in a world that desperately needs it. We believe that God has used good men and women through the earth to accomplish his purposes and that he will continue to do so in the future.

C.S. Lewis, writing from a Christian perspective, once observed: "It is not for us to say who, in the deepest sense, is or is not close to the spirit of Christ. We do not see into men's hearts. We cannot judge, and are indeed forbidden to judge. It would be wicked arrogance to say that any man is, or is not, a Christian." The issue before us is, of course, broader than Christianity or monotheism. There is a risk associated with learning something new about someone else. New insights always affect old perspectives, and thus some rethinking, rearranging, and restructuring of our worldview are inevitable. When we look beyond a man or woman's color or ethnic group or social circle or church or synagogue or mosque or creed or statement of belief, when we try our best to see them for who and what they are, children of the same God, something good and worthwhile happens within us, and we are thereby drawn into a closer union with the God of us all.

A Kantian Universalist Response

Reflections on Bill Moyers's "Genesis and the Millennium"

SABRINA P. RAMET*

For the religious, nothing is so certain, so beyond dispute, as articles of faith. Science, history, and art may have their "truths," but these are often more easily challenged than tenets of one's own religion. For the religious believer—and 95 percent of Americans describe themselves as believers—the core of the faith provides the lenses, as it were, through which the world is seen. Now that core may be defined differently by different members of the same faith; but the basic point is nonetheless valid.

Bill Moyers recognizes this characteristic of religious faith and wants to affirm the principle of tolerance against those who would demonize those subscribing to other views and who would affirm the doctrine of "no tolerance for error." Who, after all, will define what constitutes error, if not the self-declared patriarchs of Universal Truth? As Moyers wisely puts it, "to be furious in religion, is to be furiously irreligious." Indeed, it does not require profound knowledge of the Bible to realize that the parable of the "good Samaritan," the Sermon on the Mount (remember "Blessed are the peacemakers?"), and Christ's admonition to an angry crowd, "Let

---

*SABRINA P. RAMET is Professor of International Studies at the University of Washington. She has lived for extended periods of time in England, Germany, Austria, Yugoslavia, Japan, and the United States. Her many books include *Nihil Obstat: Religion, Politics, and Social Change in East-Central Europe and Russia* and *Whose Democracy?: Nationalism, Religion, and the Doctrine of Collective Rights in Post-1989 Eastern Europe*. She has also edited or coedited numerous volumes and has written articles for *Foreign Affairs, World Politics, Slavic Review, Orbis, Problems of Post-Communism,* and *Journal of Church and State,* among others.

him who is without sin cast the first stone," are not incidental
and incongruous asides but emphatic affirmations, on Christ's
part, of the central importance of tolerance.

When would-be Christians seek to intensify the discrimi-
nation again gays and lesbians, they should understand that
the parable of "the good Samaritan" applies also to "the good
homosexual," as it does likewise to "the good transsexual,"
"the good non-Christian," or "the good atheist." Indeed, dis-
crimination is also contrary to everything for which this country stands—as borne out in the writings of Jefferson, Madison,
Paine, and others. For without tolerance, there can be no individual autonomy and without autonomy, there can be no
freedom. German socialist Rosa Luxemburg is famous for
having declared, on one occasion, that true freedom can only
consist in the freedom to think differently—a view seconded,
incidentally, by John Stuart Mill.

Tolerance is an essential condition for civil society—but
tolerance cannot be blind. Respect for the harm principle—
for the principle that my freedom of action ends where harm
is done to others—and the principle of fundamental human
equality (a tenet of both the Christian tradition and classical
liberalism) dictate that some things are not deserving of tolerance. Certainly, most of us would recoil at the notion that
there should be tolerance for genocide and mass rape, and by
the same virtue, the benefits of tolerance cannot be thought to
extend to hate speech, to chauvinism, or to any willful acts of
inflicting harm on others. Nihilism is scarcely a necessary
component of liberalism; in fact, it is not even a *possible* component of liberalism, since it is, on the contrary, as incompatible with liberalism as it is with Christianity. As the
eighteenth-century German philosopher Immanuel Kant
urged, freedom should be understood, in the first place, as the
freedom to live in harmony with the categorical imperative,
the imperative of universalizability.[1]

Religion and morality are not the same thing. One can be
religious without being moral, and one can be moral without
being religious. And religion is about much more than just
morality, in any case. Among other things, religion is also
about rituals, about the supernatural, about the authority of
God or gods, and often about obedience.

---

1. My paraphrase: Act always in such a way that if everyone acted as
you are acting, the world would be a better place.

It is here, on the subject of obedience, that I often reflect on the story, in the book of Genesis, about God commanding Abraham to take his son Isaac, tie him to an altar, and slay him. From my point of view, it appears that the point of this story could be that God—or at least the God imagined by the author of Genesis—is (or should be thought to be) *above*—the moral law. How different is the God of the New Testament, both from the amoral God of Genesis and from the whimsical God of Job! It is hard to imagine that the God of the New Testament could ever conceive of His will sundered from the moral law. As St. Thomas Aquinas put it, divine law and natural law (or "Right Reason," as St. Thomas puts it) are one and the same.

To this, the Christian right offers a double challenge. On the one hand, the Christian right wants to assert that it enjoys an exclusive right to prescribe substantive rules for *all* Americans—whether regarding same-sex couples or abortion or prayer in the schools or other matters—and that it is "authorized" (by God, presumably) to employ the mechanisms of the state for this purpose (thereby scuttling the principle of church-state separation, as Moyers notes). On the other hand, the Christian right also wants to uphold the notion that "correct belief" is not secondary, but primary, or—to put it another way—"if you do not accept Jesus Christ as your saviour, you cannot go to heaven." And needless to say, "correct belief" includes acceptance of the teachings of the Christian right, in other words, obedience. And so one is back to Abraham's dilemma.

Here I shall offer a bold challenge. Abraham faced a clear choice between blind obedience to authority and loyalty to the moral law (with its corollary, respect for human life). Abraham made the wrong choice, choosing blind obedience over morality. One reading of this story would have it that God Himself considered this the "wrong" choice, and that in sending His angel to stay Abraham's hand, He admitted as much, even while forgiving Abraham for having failed this test. So while the story could be read as constructing a God who valued obedience over morality, it could also be read as showing that God recognized that adherence to the principle of obedience-above-all could have morally unacceptable consequences—specifically, violation of the harm principle.

Before closing, I would like to say a few things about millennium fever. To begin with, I share Moyers's concern that some people with big imaginations may create a certain amount of havoc in this numerologically marked year. What has been lacking so far in discussions of millennial anxiety (as far as I am aware) is a basic modesty. After all, it takes an enormous amount of hubris to believe that a supernatural being would set His watch, as it were, by a human system of counting which, in any event, sets the date of Christ's birth, nominally the year "0", six years before Christ was actually born. The world may well experience dire developments in the years to come. But if so, this is much more likely to be the result of industrial pollution, irreparable damage to the stratosphere, the destruction of species and habitats, global overpopulation, and deepening global poverty than the workings of a God obsessed with round numbers used in the Christian calendar.

The Christian world—or rather, the Catholic world—was confronted with extreme peril more than 450 years ago. In 1521, Martin Luther defied the Catholic Church's injunctions at the Diet of Worms, setting off the Reformation and igniting religious wars between Catholics and Protestants. Then, in 1529, an Ottoman army laid siege to Vienna, threatening one of the bastions of Catholicism with conquest by Islam. Thrown on the defensive on two fronts, Catholics at that time might well have feared that the world, or at least *their* world, was coming to an end. But it didn't.

But—and here's the nub of it all—from the perspective of the moral law, questions about the end of the world ("the end of time") do not matter. With or without "the end of the world," the moral law is the same and the duties it imposes— to treat others as subjects, not as objects, and to behave in such a way that if everyone behaved as one is behaving, the world would be a better place—remain ever the same.

A Christian Left Response

Limitations of the Liberal Spirit: The Need for a Religious Left in the Year of Grace 2000

HAROLD WELLS*

It was delightful and stimulating to read Bill Moyers's paper, "Genesis and the Millennium." I share much of the liberal spirit which shines through these pages, and wish to say a hearty *Yes!* to much of what he is saying. Yet I suppose it is well within the range of liberality to say that the liberal spirit also needs to be supplemented with a healthy dose of "radicalism" (and a pinch of "conservatism" too). Why do I play with labels that seem to slot people into pigeon-holes? It seems so illiberal to do so. Yet the labels say something about traditions and communities of thought, and it has become impossible to think critically without them.

On first reading Bill Moyers's paper I asked myself what it was really about. Is it about biblical interpretation, and the rejection of fundamentalism, especially where the book of Genesis is concerned? Is it about the nonsense of millennial hysteria surrounding the year 2000? Or theodicy, in face of the suffering of the innocent? Is it about the politics of the religious right, which he finds distasteful? Or is it about inter-

*HAROLD WELLS is professor of Systematic Theology at Emmanuel College, University of Toronto, and is an ordained minister of the United Church of Canada. He served many years as a pastor of congregations in Ontario and as a missionary chaplain/lecturer in the University of Lesotho (southern Africa). His particular areas of interest in theology are political and liberation theologies; contextual methods and hermeneutics; contextual theologies, especially Canadian, African, and Korean; Wesley, Moltmann, and theologies of interreligious dialogue. He is author, coauthor, or coeditor of a number of books, most recently: *A Future for Socialism? Political Theology and the "Triumph of Capitalism,"* and *The Reconciliation of Peoples.*

religious dialogue, and the need for a pluralist approach to ultimate truth? In fact the paper contains tidbits of wisdom on all of these, sown together with admirable warmth and humor. On second reading, the paper seemed to be, on a number of different fronts, a fine expression of the liberal spirit. It is the liberal spirit which he is recommending to his hearers, and which constitutes the unity of his paper.

By "liberal spirit" I refer not to the classically liberal *laissez-faire* economics of Adam Smith (ironically, more or less the economic approach of the religious right) but, broadly, to the spirit of the eighteenth-century Enlightenment, and its philosophical legacy in our time. The Enlightenment philosophers stood against dogmatism and rigidity of every kind. They were suspicious of tradition and structures of authority, whether of church or of state. They stood for free thought, tolerance, and above all, for reason. They rightly reacted against the witch hunting, heretic burning, and religious wars that had plagued Europe for centuries, and the church's mindless rejection of the new science, and its persecution of scientists. The Enlightenment had great confidence in the power of the rational mind to find the truth and to improve the world. It was faith in progress through the exercise of autonomous human reason, the very essence of modernity. For a Christian there is much to admire in the liberative aspects of the Enlightenment. Who could wish to go back behind it to a pre-modern time? In this sense we all belong to the "liberal" tradition.

Yet today, in view of the colossal atrocities of the twentieth century, and of lurking nuclear and ecological disaster in the century ahead, we have come to doubt the modern faith in progress and the inevitability of a better world. Many of us enter the new millennium with hope, but not with optimism. In our sober "postmodern" world we are not so sure about the power of human reason to reach objective truth. The truth of postmodern thought is precisely that the truth is often the truth of the powerful. Karl Marx already knew this: "The ideas of the ruling class are in every epoch the ruling ideas."[1]

Could it be that "liberal" truth is also the truth of the powerful? Now please understand that I am not using the world "liberal" in the pejorative way that it is used by the American right wing. Rather, I am questioning the liberal spirit from the other side of the spectrum, from the left (which has affini-

---

1. Karl Marx, *The German Ideology* (1848).

ties with an older conservative tradition). The liberal spirit, in its openness and tolerance to all, may have the effect of neutralizing people in their struggles for what is right and true and just. There is a tendency not to take sides. For example, a liberal perception of the political order is that class struggle does not exist, a perception especially strong in the United States, and one that obviously serves the interest of the ruling class. This is the land of equal opportunity, is it not? Moyers may be in danger of slipping into this error. In spite of his dislike of the religious right, he does not want religion *politicized*, or communities *polarized*. One of the important insights of liberation theology is that to be "apolitical" is to be unconsciously political on the side of the status quo. The reality is that religion is inescapably political, and communities are already, *de facto*, polarized, in a situation where the gap between the rich and poor is increasing. In the United States it is still enormously disadvantageous to be black. The United States is the only nation in the "developed" world that lacks a universal medical care plan, so that about one-third of the population has no medical coverage whatsoever![2] American social security programs are at the most primitive level, child labor is on the increase, and big capital, in the pursuit of profit maximization, has an iron grip on both domestic and international public policy.[3] It is naïve to think we can avoid "polarizing the community" by holding liberal Bible studies. Of course we all hope that "you can disagree passionately with people about things that matter without surrendering your own principled beliefs or going for your neighbor's throat; that we can engage with others in serious conversation about the most deeply felt subjects . . . and truly challenge each other, teach each other and learn from each other." Yes. But to live these liberal ideals is easier for comfortable middle class people than for others whose livelihood, and whose children's health and education are at stake. The religious right needs to be countered not by a politically neutralized liberal theology, but by a *religious left*, which calls Christians to fol-

---

2. Richard J. Barnet and John Cavanagh, *Global Dreams: Imperial Corporations and the New World Order* (New York: Simon and Schuster, 1994). See also Linda McQuaig, *The Wealthy Banker's Wife: The Assault on Equality in Canada* (Toronto: Penguin Books, Canada, 1993), 17.
3. For information on child labor in the U.S., see Barnet and Cavanagh, *Global Dreams*, 80. For an analysis of American society and politics, see John K. Galbraith, *The Culture of Contentment* (Boston: Houghton and Mifflin, 1992).

low Jesus in his solidarity with those who are oppressed and poor. We should not ask people to adopt a liberal, open-minded attitude if they are black and poor, and their children stand a good (statistical) chance of being executed, perhaps innocently, in one of the last of the Western nations to practice capital punishment.

I was surprised by the title: "Genesis and the Millennium." Why not "Leviticus and Millennium?" The vision of social equality found in Leviticus 25 calls for a year of grace: for the freeing of slaves, cancellation of debt, and the restoration of land to the disinherited every fifty years. It has inspired a worldwide Jubilee movement for the forgiveness of Third World debt in the Year of Grace 2000.[4] Leviticus proclaims a fifty year sabbatical for the land as well. Linked with Luke 4:16f., Leviticus 25 delivers a powerful message for a society such as the United States, so marked by environmental abuse and gross social inequality.

But I fear it is in bad taste for me, as a Canadian, to point a finger at American society, while commenting critically on a distinguished American author. As one who identifies with the Christian democratic socialist tradition and the minority Canadian political left, I deplore the way in which the dominance of capital and the market have impoverished so many in Canada as well, and undermined the reality of democracy. Canada also suffers great social injustice, homelessness, and deterioration of health care. Canadians have a tendency to feel their country is morally superior to the United States, since we do still have universal medicare coverage, a lower infant mortality rate, a narrower gap between rich and poor; we have abolished capital punishment, enjoy gun control laws, have much lower murder rates, and so on.[5] Of course moral superiority is always foolish, and un-Christian, since it is a denial of grace. We have to recognize that the United States has a vastly different social history from ours, and the differences between us have complex historical roots. We are aware that the best, most cooperative and compassionate aspects of our society are in large measure the fruit of a vigor-

---

4. Canadian Ecumenical Jubilee Initiative, *Making a New Beginning: Biblical Reflections on Jubilee* (Toronto: CEJI, 1998).
5. See James Laxer, *The False God: How the Globalization Myth has Impoverished Canada* (Toronto: Lester Publishing, 1993); also *The Undeclared War: Class Conflict in the Age of Cyber Capitalism* (Toronto: Penguin Books Canada Ltd., 1998).

ous democratic socialism, which exerted considerable influence earlier in the twentieth century and grew in large measure out of Christian "social gospel" (i.e., religious left) inspiration. But it is a struggle today in Canada to avoid losing what has been gained, and to resist the increasing globalization (which often in practice means Americanization) of Canadian society. It will not be a polite liberal spirit, nor a depoliticized theology that will move us toward God's justice and peace. In fact, as a Canadian, I am aware of a small but courageous American political left, including an American Christian socialist tradition, which sees the need to get beyond merely neutral political theologies.[6] If we are going to "talk about God in public," we should certainly not avoid "politicizing" religion, nor evade the polarization of the community which already exists.

What I call the "liberal spirit" also shines through Moyers's comments on world religions. It is a generous spirit of openness and listening. Here again, I resonate warmly to much of what is being said. Indeed, "the world is shrunk," and in the new millennium Christians must face this and celebrate it. It is appalling that "religious discourse . . . has been dominated by the Religious Right." This dominance pertains not only to politics but to the relations among the religions. The liberal spirit serves us well here, with its emphasis on tolerance and respect for others. Indeed we must "take the scriptures back from the grip of those who assert an exclusive pipeline to God." Moyers is right to speak of what Christians can learn from the other great religions. I am appreciative of the work he has done in Asia, such as his exploration of the Chinese concept of *chi* and its significance for physical and spiritual healing.[7]

But is he in danger of falling into a "temptation" that he himself identifies: " . . . that religion gets reduced to the least common denominator, a melange of superficial and borrowed opinions that lead to relativism and even nihilism, where everybody believes everything and yet no one believes any-

---

6. See Norman Thomas, *The Choice Before Us: Mankind at the Crossroads* (New York: MacMillan, 1932); also Michael Harrington, *Socialism: Past and Future* (New York: Arcade, 1989). See comments on the American democratic socialist tradition in my book, *A Future for Socialism: Political Theology and the "Triumph of Capitalism"* (Valley Forge: Trinity Press International, 1996), 138-41.

7. Bill Moyers, *Healing and the Mind* (New York: Doubleday, 1993).

thing." A lively debate is raging among Christians today about the theology of religion, among those commonly labeled (or labeling themselves) exclusivists, inclusivists, or pluralists.[8] Moyers has clearly adopted the pluralist stance, which certainly coheres best with the liberal tradition. But perhaps here he needs to listen to his own evangelical Baptist background, and to include a dash of "conservatism" in his theological mix. "Radical" and "conservative" stances often have a peculiar affinity, especially in their distrust of the liberal tendency to blur distinctions and to posit unity and agreement where they do not really exist.

Moyers's liberal, pluralist stance in the theology of religion is evident when he writes that "we humans construct different worldviews from our different angles on reality. It can be wondrous to discover how the same world all of us inhabit appears in different forms through a kaleidoscope of perspectives. . . ." Yes. But is the Christian faith a worldview which we have constructed? What of revelation? What if the Gospel of Jesus Christ is radically given, something which appears weak and foolish to the wise and rational human mind? The apostle Paul argues precisely that, noting the appeal of the gospel to the powerless:

Consider your own call, brothers and sisters: not many of you were wise by human standards, not many were powerful, not many were of noble birth. But God chose what is foolish in the world to shame the wise; God chose what is weak in the world to shame the strong. God chose what is low and despised in the world, things that are not, to reduce to nothing things that are, so that no one might boast in the presence of God. . . .(I Cor 1:26-29)

Christians do make particular truth claims that are incompatible with rival claims found in other religions and in secular stances. They do not usually regard them as a human construct or worldview, but consider that their faith has arisen out of God's unique self-disclosure in Jesus Christ. If we interpret Christian doctrines (gospel assertions about God, Jesus Christ, the Spirit, salvation by grace, God's Reign, eternal life) as "myths," or general religious truths in story form (à la Joseph Campbell) and so relativize them in relation to the

---

8. See, for example, a recent volume including contributions from authors representing all of these stances: Leonard J. Swidler and Paul Mojzes, eds., *The Uniqueness of Jesus: A Dialogue with Paul F. Knitter* (Maryknoll: Orbis, 1997).

"myths" of all the other religions, we undermine the specific message and motivating power of Christian faith. Of course we recognize that there are mythical and legendary elements in the Bible; we do not have to choose between "fundamentalism" and mythologized theology. As I have already suggested, the Christian gospel is a radical message of grace, of hope for history, especially for all the oppressed and lowly victims of the world, because of the breaking into of history of God's Reign in the crucified Jesus, in whom God is present for the whole world. In Jesus we encounter the suffering God, the God whose love is most glorious in humiliation and lowliness. In the event of Jesus' resurrection we have, in time and space, the unique sign and promise of the vindication of the victims of history in God's coming Reign. To mythologize the gospel is to de-historicize it, de-politicize and de-radicalize it.

To regard the world religions as mythological human constructs is offensive, of course, not only to Christians, but also to Muslims, Buddhists, and others. One danger of the pluralist approach to a theology of religion is that it subtly attempts to impose its neo-Protestant monotheism upon the whole world as a kind of liberal common sense. Is this not yet another, gentler form of Western imperialism? It purports to view all the religions, including Christianity, from a superior platform above and beyond them all, and to see them all as varying forms of the same thing.[9] It is true, as Moyers says, that "all the great religions grapple with things that matter, although each may come out at a different place. . . . that each and every one of them deserves attention for the wisdom they might offer to humanity." Yes. But is it true, as Moyers says, that "each arises from within?" Most Christians believe that their faith is a gift from beyond themselves, and which calls in question all our human constructs, religious and political.

The strength of the liberal tradition is clear. We dare not leave it behind, lest we fall into mindless bigotry and authoritarianism. Moyers is an impressive representative of the liberal spirit. But the limitation of that tradition is its tendency to premature reconciliation and synthesis, its temptation to false peace.

---

9. See Lesslie Newbigin, *The Gospel in a Pluralist Society* (Grand Rapids: Eerdmans, 1989). Also, S. Mark Hiem, *Salvations: Truth and Difference in Religion* (Maryknoll: Orbis, 1995).